Seasonal Planting
in GARDEN DESIGN

A guide
to creating year-round colour and structure

Catherine Heatherington

Seasonal Planting
in GARDEN DESIGN

A guide
to creating year-round colour and structure

THE CROWOOD PRESS

CONTENTS

INTRODUCTION

Change is fundamental to natural systems, and it is the dynamism, drama and excitement of changes, from the smallest details to the overarching views, that inspire us when exploring and experiencing the landscape. Seasonal change is something to be welcomed, bringing different atmospheres and conjuring up feelings of renewal and rebirth. And yet as designers of gardens and urban spaces, we are often asked to take a more static approach with requests for an 'all-season' garden, for year-round colour, for evergreens. Taken at face value this can limit our designs, ignoring the potential of a truly seasonal garden.

We are lucky in the UK to have four seasons to work with, each with its own particular charms and challenges. Our winters are rarely cold for months on end and our summers are not yet consistently hot enough for plants to enter a dormant period – although, as I will discuss in later chapters, this may not always be the case. As well as colour we can explore textures, forms and structure, dead and dying foliage, scents and changes in mass and void. These factors contribute to the aesthetic of the design and in this book, I will discuss the many ways in which the qualities of plants can be used to enhance a genuinely seasonal successional garden.

Understanding the seasons and designing in harmony with the natural world is not only an aesthetic imperative, but it is also a necessity. Research in England (Thompson and Head, 2020), suggests that the area taken up by gardens is between four and five times as large as the total area of our national nature reserves. Gardens, therefore, are an important resource. However, with many new-build houses, the space given over to green spaces is decreasing and in addition the amount of greenery in all gardens, in the form of trees and shrubs, is also declining. Between 1998 and 2008 London lost the equivalent of 2.5 Hyde Parks every year (Thompson and Head, 2020).

All the more reason for every garden in its own small way to make some impact on the threat to biodiversity. Designing for wildlife means that we are thinking about flowering plants and seedheads, structural shrubby layers and trees, dense corridors and open spaces, and ensuring that these persist through the seasons – things which benefit the creatures in our gardens as well as the people that inhabit them.

We can also think about how our gardens can work to mitigate the climate crisis. Rather than constantly tidying up, cutting back, removing vegetation and digging to expose bare soil, a successional planting design involves keeping the ground covered and undisturbed as much as possible, thus improving water retention and allowing carbon to remain in the soil.

In the chapters that follow I explore the aesthetics of seasonal successional design, discussing the ways plants interact and complement each other over time and I consider how this approach works in accordance with nature, bringing delight to the people who visit, providing habitats for a diversity of creatures and emphasising the need for observation and flexibility, which will improve our chances to mitigate and respond to an uncertain future.

Textural frost-rimmed leaves of *Persicaria* and *Nepeta* in midwinter.

CHAPTER 1

SETTING THE SCENE

In our gardens, we are constantly performing a balancing act, accommodating nature and horticulture. For some, this means keeping nature under control but others of us want to let nature into our gardens to create new habitats. In this time of climate crisis, it is essential to consider how gardens can be created to be sustainable and thus become a source of joy to their human visitors, while also being of benefit to the wildlife that visits and inhabits these spaces.

In this book the term 'seasonal succession' describes a planting design approach that ensures changing layers of interest throughout the year. The aim is to create waves of colour, form and texture and a fluidity of contrasts between mass and void as the seasons progress. As we will explore in Chapter 7, the bonus of this approach is that it also encourages and supports invertebrates, birds and other creatures.

Sustainability with respect to hard landscaping is a subject for an entire book, but the changing climate also has a bearing on our choices of plants and below you will find some of the recent research and suggestions from people working in the field. As the climate crisis proceeds many native plants will struggle to survive and the range of certain species is likely to move northwards to be replaced in the south by plants from Europe that are better able to cope with the new conditions. James Hitchmough (2020) points out that silver birch is already struggling in Southern England and my unscientific, personal observation during the high temperatures and drought in 2022 noted that it was indeed showing signs of stress, as were hawthorn and native viburnum. It is not possible to say with any certainty which plants will cope with the unpredictable, changing conditions and this makes it more important than ever to observe what is happening in the world around us and to experiment with a diverse range of species in our designed gardens and landscapes.

Learning from Nature

This chapter begins with a discussion of just a few of the many different habitats found in nature and examines how the behaviour of these plant communities through the seasons can inform our design. What we describe as the natural world around us has been influenced by human behaviour for thousands of years and all the plant communities discussed here continue to be affected to a lesser or greater extent by our actions.

Ecological Succession

Before looking at how we can learn from nature when designing for the changing seasons it is worth understanding the meaning of ecological succession and how it differs from seasonal succession. *Encyclopaedia Britannica* defines ecological succession as 'the process by which the structure of a biological community evolves over time' (Thompson, n.d.). A community comprises plants, animals, fungi, microbes: organisms below ground as well as above. Succession is characterised as either primary or secondary. The former takes place when starting from a lifeless landscape that may have resulted from catastrophic destruction such as volcanic eruption or glacier retreat (Rafferty, n.d.). Secondary succession occurs when a community is destroyed, for example, by fire, but where some life remains: after a fire a seed bank is waiting in the ground to germinate when conditions are favourable. In this time of climate crisis, disruptive and cataclysmic events will happen more frequently, and any discussion of succession must take account of anthropogenic factors.

Although change, including unpredictable change, is a fundamental part of succession, a progression of increasing complexity can be observed as an ecosystem develops. Secondary succession usually begins with pioneer species – annuals, followed by grasses and perennials. These establish over several years, gradually altering the soil structure and creating shade, before the appearance of shrubby vegetation, birch and pine, and then, eventually, broad-leafed trees like oak. After as much as 150 years, if no major disturbances occur, a stable mature forest may be established – a climax community (Rafferty, n.d.).

A small-scale example of secondary succession brought about by human action can be observed in post-industrial landscapes, which I will explore in more detail in Chapter 6. Industrial activity over years pollutes the landscape and destroys vegetation and wildlife but when the site is abandoned and dereliction takes hold, a new ecosystem begins to evolve. The starting point for this community may be very different from what was there before; new substrates will be present supporting a limited, but often unusual, range of plants. However, over years, the stages of succession gradually establish to create new communities. Nevertheless, it is important to remember that

The forest floor in autumn.

succession is also dependent on animals as part of the biological community. Grazing by large herbivores and rooting up of plants by animals, such as wild boar, would in the past have been part of a successional community (Tree, 2018). These creatures are not found in today's industrial wastelands, so any talk of 'rewilding' gardens and landscapes must consider the implications of this, as we will see in Chapter 7.

Ecologists also talk of cyclic succession in established communities. This is when some of the species in the community die or become dormant before re-emerging on a cyclical basis, maybe annually or over a period of years (BD Editors, 2019). In gardens, planning for dormancy is part of the challenge of designing for seasonal succession. We are less likely to plan for the death of a plant species, although this is what we are doing when using annuals and short-lived or self-seeding perennials.

As designers and garden makers, examining and observing ecological communities can inform our thinking when creating seasonal successional planting schemes. We can learn from how the communities are structured, the plant forms and how they change through the seasons, together with the vertical layering taking place. This does not mean you are restricted to choosing the same plants you observe within an ecological community, although you may wish to include one or two. Instead select species that behave in a similar way and have similar characteristics.

Trees

Trees form a key component of many diverse plant communities, support a multitude of wildlife, and play a crucial role in life below ground. They occur, singly, in small groups, in woodlands and forests. They may be young saplings, mature specimens or in a period of senescence at the end of their lives. They also transform light and shade and in this way above all, they are closely linked to the seasons and the passage of time.

Form and Texture

In winter the form of a deciduous tree and the textures of its bark are its defining visual characteristics. In late autumn and early spring these qualities are enhanced by low sunlight filtering through to the woodland floor. The shape of trees such as oak, with its curved and gnarled low branches, is perhaps seen to best advantage in the winter and the ridges and furrows of the swirling bark of the sweet chestnut is revealed as it catches the light. Trees can inspire us to value dormancy in our gardens and when choosing a tree and where to site it, we can consider how best to work with the available light through the seasons.

In woodlands, dead and fallen trees create new habitats: invertebrates shelter in and feed on rotting wood and opportunistic plants, such as silver birch, drop seed into fallen trunks. The fruiting bodies of

Low autumn light shining through pine trees (© Ellie Mindel).

A shrubby understorey survives in the semi-shade beneath the distinctive branches of an oak tree.

Beneath

In a garden it is more likely that trees will be planted singly or in small groups, but it is still useful to observe the understorey and woodland floor to learn about how plants behave in these communities. Light levels are one factor in determining what can grow. In the spring when there are no leaves on the trees, the light penetrates the canopy of branches and from January through to June plants such as snowdrops, wood anemones, bluebells and wild garlic take advantage of this. As the trees come into full leaf the light levels are reduced and shade-loving ferns and woodrush take over from the earlier bulbs. Other plants that cope with shady conditions are cuckoo pint and celandine. The former loses its leaves soon after flowering in spring, all but disappearing, only to become more conspicuous later with its spire of bright orange berries. Celandine also disappears after flowering, leaving space for other species to take over. A word of warning, however – both these plants can be invasive in gardens and so should be introduced with care.

Shrubs and small trees, such as hazel, elder, dogwood, butcher's broom, holly and birch, form the understorey of the woodland and often look rather straggly if they are struggling towards the light, but where there are gaps in the tree cover, they provide a valuable middle layer in the plant community. Climbers

fungi appear in autumn amongst the leaf litter and dead branches, whilst, in some conditions, lichens gradually colonise the trees. Whether dead or living, the shapes of the trunks and branches add drama to a winter landscape.

When in leaf, the form of an individual tree changes as the canopy emerges. Early leaves allow light to filter through, creating shimmers and dapples on the woodland floor. As summer progresses, the branches are less prominent and the overall shape of the tree takes precedence. These are the forms we use as designers: round, spreading, columnar, pyramidal, conical, weeping. We can also learn from traditional management techniques in woodland; coppicing and pollarding create eye-catching silhouettes that change through the seasons.

In exposed conditions the form of trees is affected by the prevailing weather conditions: wind sculpts trees into dramatic shapes. It is unlikely that we can replicate these shapes in design, but it is worth considering how to bring a natural drama at different times of the year through judicious pruning and training.

Intermingling ground cover on the woodland floor.

Scenes from one woodland taken in winter and spring: snowdrops (top), garden escape narcissus (bottom left) and native bluebells (bottom right) succeed one another, to be followed later by ferns and *Luzula*.

make the transition between this layer and the canopy: honeysuckle, old man's beard, wild rose and ivy scramble up slender branches towards the light.

In autumn, as light again penetrates, ferns, such as bracken, die back, turning a rusty brown and revealing cushions of bright green moss. There might also be fruits and nuts to crunch underfoot amongst the leaf litter.

Hedgerows, Verges and Woodland Edges

Hedgerows may have originated from human activity in the bronze age as land was cleared for fuel, building and farming, leaving strips of woodland to mark boundaries (The Royal Society for the Protection of Birds, n.d.). They can be thought of as emulating what would once have been a natural transition between woodland and grassland. New hedges were planted from Roman times onwards and this increased during the eighteenth century with the introduction of the Enclosures Act (Woodland Trust, 2013). It was after the Second World War that hedgerows began to be removed, creating large fields that were easier to cultivate as farming was increasingly mechanised. There is now an understanding of the importance of hedges for wildlife and to protect soils, but there is still a long way to go to improve and extend our hedgerows and to ensure that they are managed appropriately (Woodland Trust, 2013).

Tapestries

A mixed native hedge of hazel, dogwood, hawthorn, guelder rose, field maple, spindle and holly can provide interest throughout the year. In spring leaves begin to unfurl – the many shades of green gradually changing as the season progresses. In May there is the white blossom of hawthorn followed by the flowers of the guelder rose. As summer proceeds the form of the hedge itself is a backdrop to the vegetation at its base. Autumn brings colourful leaves (the yellow field maple, crimson dogwood and guelder rose) and berries (the orange/pink of the spindle and the red of hawthorn and guelder rose). Finally in winter the bare, interlocking branches have their own presence and holly displays bright red berries against dark green leaves, before dormancy is broken with distinctive hazel catkins at the beginning of the new year.

In addition to the shrubs in the hedge, there are the climbers that scramble through the branches, twining around to reach the light. As in the woods, honeysuckle, old man's beard, dog rose and hop as well as ivy are all part of the diversity of the tapestry.

In a small garden it is not always possible to plant a hedge or to allow it the space necessary to display the many seasonal changes. However, we can learn from the intermingling tapestry of hedgerows to create a diverse palette of shrubs and learn how to manage them for optimum interest.

Edges

It is especially useful to understand the edges of woodland and the verges beside hedges when designing for seasonal succession. These habitats are like many spaces found in gardens: semi-shade under a tree, dry conditions next to a wall or fence, planting around larger shrubs and the layering of perennials and grasses.

A matrix of intermingling species on the coast in Wales, taken in early summer.

As with the woodland floor, in spring when light can reach the ground, bluebells, wild garlic, anemones and primroses thrive. Along the back of the verge and the edge of the wood, there are plants that prefer semi-shade. These include asplenium, dead nettle, stinking hellebore, betony, bugle, foxglove, spreading bell-flower, woodruff and red campion. The statuesque alexanders, *Smyrnium olusatrum*, and the more deli-cate cow parsley, *Anthriscus sylvestris,* also like the hedgerow habitat. The tall umbels cast shadow over the lower growing flowers – the primroses, violets and other back-of-the-verge species. By July the dramatic yellow green of the alexanders and the froth of creamy lace is over, to be replaced by dead stems and seedheads.

The diversity of a verge in limestone hills in Yorkshire.

The Diversity of Edges

Roadside verges provide rich diverse habitats for flora and fauna. Some are the remnants of ancient hay meadows and others once edged drover's paths that would have been grazed by the livestock passing along (Plantlife, 2017). Many verges now are in constant flux, disturbed by car tyres, excavation and building works. Plantlife has researched the diversity of vegetation found in our verges and identifies six different habitats: grassy, disturbed, wooded, salted, ditches and hedgerows. Within these habitats there are also different soil conditions affecting the mix of vegetation they support (Plantlife, 2017). Grassy or heathy verges can be wet or dry and soils range from acid to alkaline. Disturbed verges usually support those cornfield annuals that need disturbance to germinate. Also found by the side of roads, salted verges have received the run-off from the roads treated for snow and ice in winter and support a range of halophytic plants. Ditches are habitats for emergent plants that cope with wet but not submerged conditions, and finally, hedgerows support a range of species that are happy at the base of taller shrubby plants.

Plantlife's research shows that just over 50 per cent of the UK flora is found in these hedges, verges and ditches (2017). However, many species are under threat: British wildflowers prefer a soil low in nutrients but pollution from the air and from vehicle exhausts is increasing the nitrogen in the soil and encouraging more invasive vegetation such as bramble, nettle, creeping buttercup and Yorkshire fog, which then crowd out other species. Particularly at risk are tufted vetch, lady's bedstraw, bugle, white campion and greater knapweed (Plantlife, n.d.-b).

An ancient drove road in North Yorkshire. The hedge is a mass of hawthorn blossom and cow parsley edges the track.

Meadows and Grassland

A traditional meadow is a perfect example of an inter-lacing matrix of vegetation in which different species grow up and through each other creating a supporting framework of stems and leaves. Like the edges dis-cussed above, lower growing plants appear earlier in the year and are then shaded out by taller perennials and grasses. Colours change through the seasons as different species dominate, but the overall effect is one of dots of many colours against a harmonious green background. Often the form of the individual flower is less important than the mass of moving colours. Nevertheless, there are species that rise above the others and show off their distinctive forms: the striking shapes of the larger umbellifers and the spires of fox-gloves, mullein and purple loosestrife tower above the sea of flowers and grasses.

Wildflower meadows are mown and raked in the autumn leaving the landscape exposed and sometimes featureless. However, watching low sunlight falling across grassland on undulating or sloping ground immediately makes clear the value of creating land-forms to add autumn and winter interest to a garden. These sculptural elements can be designed to catch the light in different ways throughout the day and to create interest. The dormant period is to be valued as a time of calm before the turbulence of the meadow reasserts itself.

Knapweed and grasses in a meadow on the Gower Peninsula in Wales.

Moors and Heathlands

Heathland is characterised by infertile and well-drained soils whereas moorland, more often found in upland regions, is usually wetter, and sometimes peaty. Both landscapes have been modified over the centuries by human actions and grazing by domestic and wild animals (Woodland Trust, n.d.).

Getting down close to the ground reveals the interlacing matrix of vegetation on a moor or heath, but from a more expansive vantage point the landscape often appears to be a tapestry of colour with large blocks of low shrubs and grasses occasionally interspersed by trees such as birch, rowan, willow and Scots pine. If these landscapes were not cut and grazed, the tree cover would gradually increase.

Heathland plants include heather, bracken and gorse and the colour palette changes through the seasons from greens and bright yellow gorse, through swathes of purple heathers to rusty, purple browns of dying bracken. These dramatic changes of colour are also evident on moorlands where, at different times of the year, there may be masses of white feathery cotton grass or lurid green mosses, shrubby bilberries or juniper, stiff rushes, or sedges. Interlacing within these visibly dominant colour blocks on both heath and moor are smaller dots of flowers such as bog asphodel or one of the many native orchids.

Meadows and verges demonstrate how mosaics of grasses and perennials interlace and support each other. The heathland and moorland habitats show us how to incorporate blocks of successional colour into this interlacing matrix and how to introduce low-growing shrubs and the vertical accents of small trees to give structure to a more uniform ground layer. I will return to this in Chapter 3.

Heather, bracken and gorse form a tapestry on heathland in Suffolk.

Water

Many water plants die back completely in winter and therefore it is important to consider the dormant period in the design of ponds, bog gardens and water courses. This lack of vegetation is not a problem when considering the water itself; reflections bring light and movement and rocks and pebbles add structure. It is the emergent plants and those on the edges that are more of a challenge for the designer. Many can grow quite large in one season and then die back in an unsightly mass. Vertical elements such as reeds, rushes and irises collapse and disappear leaving the ground plane exposed. In some cases, ponds and lakes are surrounded by trees and shrubby vegetation creating an aesthetically attractive frame for the water in winter. Falling leaves decaying at the bottom of the pond provide food for invertebrates but, if allowed to accumulate, may eventually cause ponds to silt up. In

contrast with the verticality of mature trees, open water in winter is an invitation to appreciate the horizontality of the landscape and the sky above.

In rocky landscapes and on slopes, the edges of ponds and streams include smaller habitats: crevices, damp shingle and pebbles, tumbling rocks, a single overhanging tree. The plants taking advantage of these spaces can inform our design and add structure and evergreen interest to the winter garden. One such is the hart's tongue fern, always green but also providing new interest in spring and summer with its unfurling bright green fronds.

It can also be useful to observe which plants are thriving in local wildlife ponds. Marsh marigold is particularly valuable in design and for wildlife because it comes into leaf and flowers in early spring, and water forget-me-not and brooklime both flower for months over the summer, the latter often keeping its leaves into the winter.

Winter reflections in Loch Fyne in Scotland.

One of the world's rare chalk rivers in Norfolk, taken in November. The dead stems of willowherb and meadowsweet line the banks.

I will explore the native and non-native plants and their benefits for wildlife in Chapter 7, but it is worth mentioning here that non-native species can become invasive in garden ponds and some are banned from sale (WWT, n.d.) (Gardeners' World, n.d.).

Shore

Plants thrive even in most inhospitable places; those on shores and cliffs must cope with fierce salt winds and often rocky, infertile conditions. In some situations, they may have to survive being submerged and in hot summers they bake in the exposed landscape. Many species are low growing, hugging the sand or the shingle, but where a bushy shrub takes a precarious hold, smaller species find a little sheltered space beneath or behind it. In this way groups of plants gradually expand. Nevertheless, the shore is usually a place of space – widely spread vegetation or mats of ground-hugging species.

Verbascum in winter (top) and summer (bottom) and *Crambe* in summer (bottom right – upper) and winter (bottom right – lower) on a Suffolk beach.

When thinking about garden design, we can learn from the small communities that have grown up through the years, or the shore itself can be an inspiration for a gravel garden or for those planted on infertile substrates. Taller species that cope with salt winds include gorse and broom as well as sea buckthorn, *Hippophae rhamnoides*, with its silvery leaves and bright orange berries. The accompanying photo shows two shoreline scenes. In winter we can appreciate the skeleton structures of *Verbascum* and the grey corpses of *Crambe maritima*. Throughout the summer, mats of grey-green *Silene uniflora* are dotted with white flowers and the *Crambe* is transformed into mounds of white with huge, wavy-edged blueish leaves. The yellow *Verbascum* still provides the vertical accents, but there are also waves of pinkish-red *Centranthus ruber* that seeds itself into rocks and crevices.

The Pattern of Landscape Revisited

The Pattern of Landscape by landscape architects Sylvia Crowe and Mary Mitchell (1988) remains invaluable more than thirty years after publication. It explains how to read the landscape and to understand the ways in which it has come to be as it is today. The world around us is a product of change over different temporal and spatial scales. Geological change, for example, is clear in the form of mountain and valley, erosion and deposition. We see anthropological change in the destruction of forests, in mining sites, or in the contrasts between ploughed fields and woodland. There is also cyclical change: hourly tidal movements, occasional flooding or fire, and the changing colours and forms of the days and the seasons.

Designers can gain inspiration from observing landscape patterns: the network of crevices in rocks; the meandering rivulets in sand and mud; the textural contrasts of geological formations and grazed grass; the juxtapositions of vertical and horizontal forms where trees and agriculture meet. And these patterns change with the seasons – changes of light, colour and texture. Crowe and Mitchell (1988) point out that some landscapes, such as deserts and canyons, only reveal their forms at sunrise and sunset when the low light transforms them into dramatic sculptures. They go on to explain:

'In distant landscapes colouring depends almost entirely on light and atmosphere, but in the foreground and middle distance the colours of rock, soil and vegetation strike the dominant note. Often their juxtaposition gives vivid contrasts' (Crowe and Mitchell, 1988, p.43).

Ancient terraces of olives create repeated horizontal and vertical patterns through the exposed rock in an agricultural landscape in Spain.

In Cumbria an ancient hawthorn embodies the force of the wind in its extreme form, allowing us to read the weather conditions that affect this landscape.

The Climate Crisis and Diversity

As the climate crisis proceeds it is up to us all to design, build and manage our gardens and landscapes in a way that is as beneficial as possible for the environment. Although there is no one blueprint to follow, any book about planting design needs to consider what the changing climate might mean for plants and wildlife, especially as gardens can help to mitigate some of the effects – in fact the Royal Horticultural Society (RHS) suggests that currently the role they could play in the future is underestimated (Webster *et al.*, 2017). We can also observe and share information, keep up to date with new research and learn from what is happening in the natural world.

It is worth summarising the detailed report, *Gardening in a changing climate*, produced by the RHS (2017), both to look at the implications and to think about what we as gardeners, garden lovers and designers can do. The RHS outlines the key implications as follows:

- An extended growing season resulting in early flowering and late leaf colouring.
- More likelihood of extreme weather conditions – in particular, extreme rainfall may damage plants and cause nutrients to be washed out of the soil.
- Possibilities for growing a different range of plants.
- Periods of drought.
- Warmer conditions that exacerbate the spread of pests and diseases.
- Suitability of trees planted today for the future climate.

The Society of Garden Designers (SGD) also considers how we can create more sustainable gardens. What follows draws on the reports produced by both the SGD (2022), (Bailey and Wilkinson, 2023) and the RHS (Webster *et al.*, 2017). A useful website, Climate Positive Design, helps designers take a look at the resources available and provides tools to measure the embodied carbon in designs (Climate positive design, 2023).

Designers Sylvie and Patrick Quibel have created a dynamic planting scheme with a diversity of species of perennials, grasses and climbers at the *Jardin Plume* in France.

Make Your Living Space Greener and Choose a Diverse Range of Plants

If you are reading this book, you probably already want to make your living space greener. Trees and other plants can help reduce carbon dioxide in the atmosphere and greening spaces such as front gardens can reduce run-off and flash flooding. Many plants can also help mitigate pollution (Traverso, 2020).

When choosing trees and shrubs with longevity in mind, having a varied selection makes it more likely that some will survive adverse conditions. It is also worth remembering that if plants flower earlier due to changes in climate, the association between the availability of nectar and the presence of pollinators is disrupted; therefore, choosing a diverse range of species may help to mitigate this.

The following ideas can help in greening your living space:

- Avoid paving over front gardens.
- Plant trees.
- Look at what is already growing healthily in the garden and consider how you can keep these plants.
- Think about creating green roofs and planting up walls and fences. This can create microclimates and help reduce heat.

This small garden, designed by the author, makes the most of the different conditions in an urban situation. Shade-loving species are planted beneath the mature tree and there is a focus on texture and form.

- Source plants with a low carbon footprint – grown locally or in the UK.
- Use conifers, which are especially good for trapping pollution because of their small leaf size and shape (Doick, 2023).
- Select a diverse range of plants for pollinators and especially focus on those that flower early and late in the season.
- Mow the lawn less frequently to encourage flowering species amongst the grass.
- Be aware that as climate change progresses, it is likely that the species of trees that will thrive will be those that at present have a range further south (Hitchmough, 2020). For example, deciduous oaks may eventually be replaced with the evergreen *Quercus ilex*, which is already establishing in the UK.

Conserve Water

Gardens need water and, with increasing drought in the summer, the need to conserve water is paramount:

- Introduce water storage and capture measures.
- Consider including rain and bog gardens.
- Choose plants that can cope with periods of drought.

- Mulch to retain water in the soil.
- Use hard landscaping materials that are compliant with Sustainable Urban Drainage Systems (SuDS).

Avoid Using Pesticides and Chemicals and Never Use Peat-Based Products

Peatlands are the largest UK carbon store and soak up rainwater, helping to reduce flood risk (Plantlife, n.d.-c). There are many alternatives to peat available and by choosing these and avoiding the indiscriminate use of pesticides and chemicals in our gardens, we can help to create habitats for wildlife rather than destroy them (*see* Chapter 7).

Practising Integrated Pest Management can also reduce the need for chemicals and pesticides and keep the spread of diseases to a minimum (Department of Agriculture Environment and Rural Affairs, n.d.). The following points can also help:

- Use biological controls and mechanical methods.
- Practise good plant husbandry.
- Make sure you practise good plant biosecurity.
- Where possible buy plants grown in the UK to avoid bringing pests into the country.
- Reduce the expansion of invasive species by avoiding the use of any cultivated plants that may escape into the wild and have an adverse effect.

Value the Soil

Soil composition and structure determine what we can grow; good soil husbandry can help to create species-rich gardens and, as a bonus, healthy soil is a significant carbon sink.

- Leave fallen leaves to compost naturally.
- Include compost heaps and wormeries.
- Avoid modifying soils except with materials found on site, such as crushed brick or stone.
- Avoid leaving exposed bare soil.
- Try a no-dig gardening system (*see* Chapter 6).
- Use mulches, including green manures, to protect the soil surface and improve the organic content (*see* Chapter 8).
- Protect the soil during any building works.

Reduce, Reuse and Recycle

Even in small gardens we can play a part in reducing the carbon footprint by reducing the use of resources that are brought in, encouraging the use of sustainable materials and avoiding waste being sent to landfill. The following ideas are just a few of the many ways you can reduce your carbon footprint:

- When creating a new garden, retain existing trees and other plants.
- Reuse materials and seasonal items.
- Recycle waste products.
- Get creative in the ways in which you recycle materials.
- Swap plants and seeds with other gardeners.
- Compost garden waste and leaves.
- Use existing hard landscaping materials to create substrates.
- Choose new materials that are available locally and that are sustainably produced.
- Choose long-lasting materials where possible and think about how they will be recycled at the end of their life.
- Think about how materials can be reused or repaired in the long term.
- Never use artificial grass unless as an alternative to tarmac or concrete and check its end-of-life destiny.

Gabions are filled with reclaimed materials to create a wall in Ballast Point Park in Sydney, designed by McGregor Coxall.

A mound of recycled broken brick used as a substrate in John Little's garden in Essex.

Increase Biodiversity

Plants and animals, insects and invertebrates, fungi and ferns – all are working together to create the ecosystems we value and our gardens should be part of this (Heatherington and Johnson, 2022). Many of the points outlined above contribute to this and Chapter 7 includes detailed information about creating sustainable habitats in the garden.

Take a Long-Term Approach

Older gardens have a greater potential to sequester carbon and provide a wider diversity of habitats:

- Think about the longevity of the plants you choose for the garden.
- Try to leave existing, thriving habitats undisturbed.
- Plan for how the garden might be used in the future, as the owners' lives change.

Many of the items discussed above are useful to remember when designing a successional garden: sustainability should be first and foremost in any gardener's mind. However, it is possible to draw out one important theme – the much-used mantra 'right plant, right place'. In addition to being mindful of the need to enhance biodiversity and reduce waste, if plants are chosen appropriately for the soil, the aspect, the climate and the garden owner then they are more likely to thrive and to earn their keep in a seasonal successional design.

Choosing Plants with the Climate Crisis in Mind

Research and experimentation are ongoing about which plants will thrive in years to come; but it makes sense to choose plants for their resilience. It is too easy to say that for hot, dry summers we should choose Mediterranean species; many of these will not be happy when faced with mild, wet winters, especially on heavy soils where their roots may become waterlogged for long periods. Researchers at the RHS and the University of Sheffield (University of Sheffield, 2020) have shown that plants with less showy flowers are more resilient to changes in climate such as flooding and drought. These plants benefit from putting less energy into creating the smaller blooms and thus are more tolerant of stress. One of the plants studied was *Primula vulgaris*, the native primrose. This performed well when compared with other highly cultivated hybrids. However, the research showed that this was not just a case of a native plant being the most resilient; one cultivar, *Primula* 'Cottage Cream' that looks very like a primrose, was better able to withstand stress than the native cowslip, *Primula veris*. The researchers call on plant breeders to focus on these findings, especially when considering producing plants that can cope with rapidly oscillating changes in conditions from wet to dry (University of Sheffield, 2020).

So how can we choose plants for a resilient, sustainable and successional garden? Dr Eleanor Webster makes some suggestions for species that cope with extreme conditions in her article for the *Garden Design Journal* (2017). She suggests a slow-growing shrub, the purple-leafed *Cotinus coggygria* 'Royal Purple', that can withstand strong winds in exposed situations. It can adjust the amount of moisture it takes from the soil, transpiring more after heavy rain but reducing water uptake in dry conditions. She also gives the example of a tree that can cope with strong winds and tolerate both wet and dry conditions, *Amelanchier* × *grandiflora* 'Robin Hill'. Another shrub that prefers sun but can also cope with changes in moisture is *Cornus alba* 'Siberica', with its bright red stems adding drama to the winter garden. All of these are invaluable for seasonal interest, creating a backbone to the design and providing colour in at least two seasons of the year.

Although I have questioned whether Mediterranean plants can survive long, wet winters, research into the effects of flooding on four such plants (King *et al.*, 2012), *Stachys byzantina*, *Cistus* × *hybridus*, *Lavandula angustifolia* 'Munstead' and *Salvia officinalis* has given some interesting preliminary results. All the plants survived a seventeen-day winter flood but the combination of flooding and high heat in summer was not so benign: the *Stachys* and *Lavandula* coped much better than the other two plants. Both are worth using in a design for seasonal succession; they provide a silver or grey-green leafed presence at the front of the border throughout the year and purple flowers in summer. It is worth experimenting with cultivars of these species such as *Stachys byzantina* 'Big Ears'.

James and Helen Basson of Scape Design have included *Euphorbia rigida*, lavender and almond trees in their Mediterranean gravel garden (© MMGI/Marianne Majerus).

If summers begin to get really dry in the south of the UK, plants may experience periods of dormancy, changing colour to silver, brown and gold much earlier in the year than we are used to. We can learn from nurserymen and designers like Olivier Filippi, discussed in Chapter 6, and James and Helen Basson (2017), who explain that we might need to embrace steppe- and prairie-style gardens in place of the English lawn and flower borders. In these schemes tall grasses add structure and accents through the year, weaving around low-growing, domed sub-shrubs. A wilder look can be achieved by allowing annuals and perennials to self-seed amongst shrubs. The Bassons (2017) suggest using the feathery fountain-like grass, *Stipa calamagrostis*, as well as *Ampelodesmos mauritanica*, although the latter is only suitable for poor, well-drained soils. The low mounds of pink and white flowered, semi-evergreen *Dorycnium hirsutum* and *D. suffruticosum* give a static structure to the scheme and taller evergreens such as *Phillyrea angustifolia*

f. *rosmarinifolia* and *Bupleurum fruticosum* provide height throughout the year (Basson and Basson, 2017). The former can be clipped into topiary shapes or used as hedging.

A few other examples worth considering in designing a successional garden are: the striking blue sea holly, *Eryngium × zabelii* 'Big Blue'; *Scabiosa cretica*, a low-growing semi evergreen with pink flowers and attractive seedheads; *Agastache foeniculum* with aromatic blue flowers; the silvery evergreen *Teucrium fruticans*, which has lavender-blue flowers in summer; statuesque *Stipa gigantea*; *Pennisetum alopecuroides* 'Hameln' that forms beautiful fountains of leaves and flowers and the tall maroon sedum, *Hylotelephium* 'Matrona'.

It is important to remember, however, that these are the early days of research into choosing species to withstand the climate crisis, and we can all play a part in making observations about plants' responses to different conditions over the next few years.

CHAPTER 2

DESIGN PRINCIPLES AND CHANGE

Successional planting involves layering plants in a design with the aim of extending the flowering season, providing year-round interest, and creating moments of drama through change. The beauty of a garden is partly found in its impermanence, ephemerality and surprise, and at times of regrowth. We do not want to lose these signs of change by creating static gardens full of clipped evergreens and the techniques in this book always try to bear this in mind.

In later chapters, we will explore how different design techniques and planting palettes can provide seasonal interest. However, it is important not to forget the fundamental principles of good design, and here we examine how these can be used to embrace change through the seasons and the years. These are divided into two: general principles that apply to the design of the garden as a whole, and the principles that are associated with details such as flower and leaf shape. The chapter ends with a discussion about the unique challenges of designing small gardens and considers how these spaces can also be a source of unexpected delights throughout the year.

Embracing Change – the Fundamentals

Garden and landscape design is about sculpting space; it is fundamentally a three-dimensional challenge underpinned by time. This means that the design is never finished, is always changing, there is never a point at which you can say, 'That's it, this is the garden completed exactly as I imagined it.' Some changes are predictable and cyclical, but others are unforeseen, depending on weather conditions, soils, competition, maintenance and so on. However, good design ensures that gardens can evolve with these changes and still retain their structure, drama, functionality and atmosphere.

When embracing change, it is important that the designer works with the garden owner, setting expectations and discussing the development and management of the garden from the outset. Designers should have sustainability at the forefront of their minds, and this can go hand in hand with a discussion about how the garden will evolve through the years.

Balance and Scale, Mass and Void

When considering balance in garden design the first elements to examine are the masses and the voids. Planting and built structures create the masses and open areas such as water, lawns, paths and patios are the voids; the balance, and also the tension, between these elements contributes to the atmosphere of a garden. A harmonious balance is easiest to achieve with a symmetrical design, but it is more interesting to experiment with the asymmetrical interplay of structural elements. Slopes, different heights and changes in level all affect the balance of the design, as does the density and visual strength of the masses and voids. It is useful to remember that 'the garden is a maze in which people occupy the voids and the wildlife broadly speaking inhabits the masses' (Heatherington and Johnson, 2022: p.44) and I will look at wildlife in relation to seasonal change in Chapter 7.

Balancing elements in a design also requires an understanding of scale: the size of things relative to the surrounding landscape and human visitors to the garden. When designing the planting, it is important to think about the mood that it will create. If the scale is overpowering – if the masses predominate and tower over you – then the garden can feel claustrophobic and enclosed. In contrast, if the planting is sparse and low to the ground in a large open space, you may feel exposed and vulnerable. These uneasy atmospheres can play a part in a dynamic, interesting design but it is important to understand how plants can create these effects.

When designing the planting we are balancing the relative size, density and position of the plant masses. However, seasonal and annual changes may subvert the designer's intentions. Trees and shrubs may only achieve their full potential as masses after several years, and a group of tall perennials can form a colourful block in the height of summer only to be transformed into a void when cut back in the winter. This is especially evident in the case of a meadow. Nevertheless, these changes can be embraced if consideration is given to other elements such as the changes in light and shadow, mood, energy and atmosphere.

Dense planting and a clipped yew hedge form the masses in this garden, designed by the author. These are balanced by the voids of the contemporary pond and the tiny lawn, glimpsed beyond the hedge.

Atmosphere is influenced by the density of the plants, as well as their colour and texture, and change through the year adds excitement. A perennial bed with a combination of a tall *Miscanthus* and *Veronicastrum virginicum*, lower growing *Astrantia*, *Epimedium* and *Allium* 'Purple Sensation' will spring to life in early spring with the delicate low flowers of the *Epimedium* on their wiry stems. At this point the bed is little more than a void with potential. The new bronze growth of the *Epimedium* quickly creates a low mass of cover around which the coarser textured *Allium* and *Astrantia* leaves start to appear. In late spring and early summer, the mass becomes denser and more dominant, while the *Allium* flower heads rise above in dramatic purple accents. It is then the turn of the *Veronicastrum* and eventually the *Miscanthus* to dominate: the mass is now dense, rising nearly to eye height. In the autumn, this density gradually declines and the seedheads have a semi-transparent ephemeral quality, colours become more muted, leaves die, but this amorphous mass persists well into the winter before being cut back in February – temporarily a void again.

For the garden visitor, in summer this little combination can contribute to an atmosphere of enclosure and seclusion, whilst in winter the more open aspect may allow attention to be drawn to other views in the garden or beyond the boundaries.

The colours of the brick paver path echo those of the alliums and sedums, and the repetition of the silver *Eryngium* brings a unity to this planting design by Tom Stuart-Smith.

Unity, Rhythm and Repetition

Unifying concepts and elements make a design more comprehensible and can also help to embed a garden into the landscape and create relationships with the surrounding buildings. Unity is expressed through the style of the garden, the concepts behind the design and the detailing. It may also be imposed by the site itself: the local materials, the surroundings or the *genus loci*. The style of a planting scheme may be formal, informal, naturalistic, tropical or minimal and concepts may include such ideas as gardening for wildlife, a jungle garden or an impressionist garden. The style and concept dictate the choice and combination of plants – the details of the design. When thinking about seasonal succession, some styles are easier to achieve than others. A formal garden relies on clipped evergreens, which will add structure throughout the year and the addition of perennials to bring seasonal change may disturb the clean lines, especially in the winter as they are drooping and dying. Similarly, a minimal design leaves little room for the diversity of planting that is necessary to create a truly successional scheme. At the opposite end of the spectrum, an informal or naturalistic planting design incorporates a wide range of perennials and grasses, but in order to unify the design these need to be contrasted with repeated static forms of judiciously placed shrubs and trees to add mass through the seasons.

These unifying shrubs do not need to be evergreen. Beneath the tall oak trees of Beth Chatto's woodland garden, perennials and bulbs intermingle with abandonment in a random naturalistic fashion to resemble woodlands we might see in nature. However, she has also introduced shrubs into this tapestry, such as *Deutzia*, *Buxus* and *Enkianthus campanulatus* and the repetition of these forms brings a unity and a focus to the exuberance of the informal planting scheme.

The quirky shapes of the yew form a repeated refrain running through an intermingling carpet of green at *Le Jardin d'Agapanthe*, Normandy, designed by Alexandre Thomas.

In Beth Chatto's woodland garden, the white flowers of the *Deutzia* shine in the dappled sunlight.

Creating attractive successional planting schemes is easier when selecting a wide range of species. It might seem that diversity and unity are contradictory concepts, however, there are ways in which a designer can still unify rather than clutter the garden. Simplicity is often cited as a way of unifying a design, but it is not necessary to keep things simple. In fact, when thinking about designing for sustainability and for wildlife diversity, intricacy and complexity are more important (Heatherington and Johnson, 2022). Instead of focusing on simplicity, think about how plants are grouped together, the ways in which they form masses to contrast with the voids. Placing smaller plants in repeating blocks and drifts unifies the design and gives a sense of rhythm to the planting scheme. Within these drifts ephemeral species can be specified, adding dots of

colour at certain times of the year or creating a gauzy, transparent overlay to the planting.

Repetition creates a rhythm to the design and introduces a dynamic element that leads the eye around the space. Consider the different forms, colours, habits, textures and scales of the individual plants and the plant combinations. Repeating plants across the garden creates links between the different areas. At its simplest this can be achieved by repetition of the same plant but in order to create interest, try repeating plants with the same form at different scales and with different seasons of interest. Rather than relying on clipped box or yew, for example, introduce a rounded shape through different species of *Pittosporum* and *Choisya* or *Lavandula* and *Santolina*. This also has the benefit of introducing contrasting textures, while maintaining unity through the rhythm of clipped forms.

Colours of similar tints, shades and tones can also be repeated; obviously the predominant unifying colour in any garden is green and this creates a calm backdrop, allowing you to experiment with a dynamic and diverse colour palette. However, repeating colours has the same impact as the repetition of forms. A successional combination of *Digitalis lutea*, *Phlomis russeliana*, *Achillea* 'Coronation Gold', *Aster* x *frikartii* 'Monch' and *Geranium* 'Rozanne' provides a repetition of shades of purple and yellow from May to October. Add a backdrop of *Clematis macropetala* and *C.* 'Polish Spirit' and the season is extended further.

Focal Points, Accents and Perspective

Focal points are incorporated into a design to:

- Add interest to the garden when viewed from the house or a seating area.
- Encourage movement around the garden.
- Draw the eye through the space.
- Bring the eye to rest, slowing down the exploration of the garden.
- Divert attention away from undesirable views.

Choosing a plant as a focal point requires an understanding of how it changes with the seasons: using a tree or an evergreen shrub is easy. However, there are other accent plants that can also create interesting focal points. An accent plant demands attention through its

The *Aruncus* is an ephemeral focal point for visitors crossing the stepping stones of this pond, designed by Mien Ruys in Dedemsvaart, Netherlands. Vertical slats frame the view, especially when the planting has died back in winter.

strong form, distinctive habit or the coarse texture of its leaves. Often the form or habit of a plant will persist through the seasons, even if it is deciduous. Good examples include: multi-stemmed trees such as *Amelanchier* and *Betula*; plants with a weeping or a fastigiate habit, such as *Pyrus salicifolia* 'Pendula' and *Cupressus sempervirens*; shrubs such as *Laurus nobilis* and *Ilex crenata* that can be trained into a multitude of shapes. Grasses such as *Molinia* 'Transparent' or *Miscanthus* 'Gracillimus', make dynamic accent plants, changing with the seasons from a mound of green, linear leaves, to a dramatic, semi-transparent vertical presence when the flowers, and ultimately the seedheads, dominate. Other accent plants only come into their own at certain times of the year: the spires of *Digitalis*, *Kniphofia* and *Verbascum* or the jungle leaves of *Melianthus* and *Rodgersia*. In these cases, bulbs can be added to create interest in the spring and the designer needs to consider what is visible when the accent or focal point is in its dormant period. One way is to include a winter flowering shrub, such as *Sarcococca* or *Viburnum* behind the more showy accent plant: in summer these do not compete with the seasonal focal point, quietly fading into the background.

A small garden designed by the author for RHS Wisley, seen here in early spring, when grasses, *Heuchera* and *Amelanchier* blossom add interest and colour.

A Courtyard Garden

The planting in this large courtyard garden is designed to adhere to fundamental design principles and provide interest and excitement throughout the year. The formal design includes a raised pond and low curved Corten screens that serve as foils to the delicate perennials and grasses and the more robust domed shrubs. The courtyard is enclosed by brick walls and a formal yew hedge that together frame the winter scene.

The repetition of the clipped evergreen forms of the *Pittosporum*, *Ilex*, *Sarcococca* and *Santolina* unify the planting scheme and provide structure and year-round interest, whilst the four multi-stem *Cornus* 'Eddie's White Wonder' change with the seasons: sculptural in winter, a mass of large white bracts in spring and red and purple colours in the autumn. The trees create tall masses in the garden amongst the lower growing perennials and grasses which ripple around the static clipped balls. *Digitalis* and *Thalictrum* are dotted through the planting and bulbs provide winter and spring interest.

Table 1 Plant list for courtyard garden

Perennials and grasses	Bulbs and underplanting
Achillea 'Cloth of Gold'	*Galanthus nivalis f. pleniflorus* 'Flore Pleno'
Astrantia major 'Ruby Wedding'	*Allium* 'Purple Sensation'
Dianthus carthusianorum	*Muscari latifolium*
Digitalis ferruginea	*Narcissus* 'Minnow'
Hakonechloa macra	*Nectaroscordum siculum*
Heuchera 'Lime Marmalade'	*Thalictrum delavayi*
Foeniculum vulgare 'Giant Bronze'	
Geranium macrorrhizum 'White Ness'	
Molinia 'Poul Petersen'	

Digitalis ferruginea in front of Corten screens.

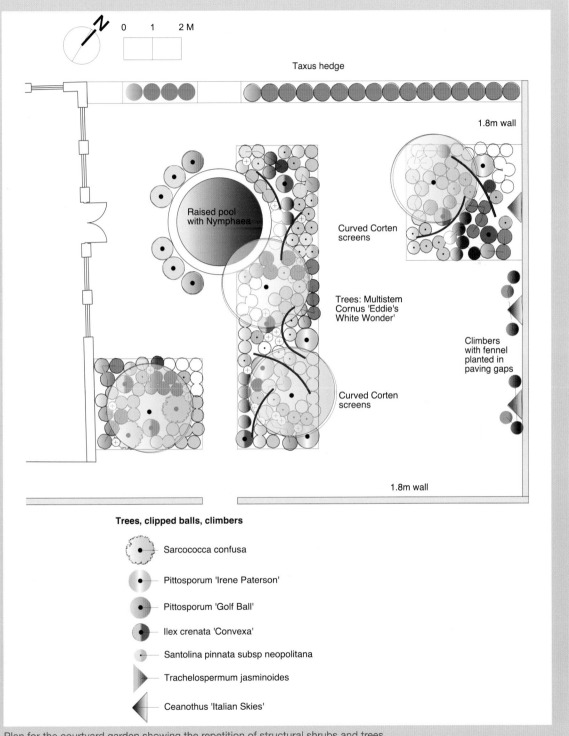

N

0   1   2 M

Taxus hedge

1.8m wall

Raised pool with Nymphaea

Curved Corten screens

Trees: Multistem Cornus 'Eddie's White Wonder'

Climbers with fennel planted in paving gaps

Curved Corten screens

1.8m wall

Trees, clipped balls, climbers

Sarcococca confusa

Pittosporum 'Irene Paterson'

Pittosporum 'Golf Ball'

Ilex crenata 'Convexa'

Santolina pinnata subsp neopolitana

Trachelospermum jasminoides

Ceanothus 'Italian Skies'

Plan for the courtyard garden showing the repetition of structural shrubs and trees.

The Details

As well as form and habit, which refer to the overall appearance of a plant, there are details such as colour, flower form, leaf texture, scent, transparency and movement that contribute to the structure, atmosphere and seasonal interest of a garden.

Flower Form

As mentioned above, form and structure are the starting points of any design but when thinking about herbaceous plants and grasses we also refer to the form of the flower itself. Colour gives drama and excitement at certain times of the year but the dead, dried flower forms last longer, even through the winter if carefully chosen. Botanists refer to the way in which flowers are arranged around a head as an inflorescence and this can change from the tight, compact shape of a bud, that opens into a flower, before drooping, dying and becoming a seedhead. All of these changes can be embraced in the design.

It is useful to look at Oudolf and Kingsbury's (1999) ways of describing perennial flower forms as a starting point to understanding the effects of different shapes and textures. They describe categories including spires, globes, plumes, umbels, daisies and screens but omit species with trumpet or bell-shaped flower heads or those with more complex double blooms. Nevertheless, some of these descriptions are particularly useful when designing a successional garden and, with that in mind, I have consolidated and adapted Oudolf and Kingsbury's list. Below we will explore spires and plumes, bobbles and spheres, dead and dying flower and seedheads and semi-transparent screens, as well as two categories that are less about the individual form of each flower and more about the overall effect of a mass of small flower heads – dots and carpets. These different shapes have evolved to aid pollination and dispersal and I will look at this in more detail when considering wildlife in the garden in Chapter 7.

Spires, spheres, trumpets and semi-transparent screens create contrasts in a flower border. The dead flower heads of the hydrangea and foxgloves will last through the winter.

Spires and plumes

Spires are a dominant presence in the garden: when planted in groups or as single plants they add a vertical element and create accents. Plumes are softer and look better when planted in blocks of one species where they give an amorphous feel to the planting scheme. They are useful as transitional or connecting plants, contrasting with the clearly defined shapes of the spires or with the rounded forms of shrubs.

At the *Jardin Plume*, designed by Patrick and Sylvie Quibel, the dramatic pink plumes of *Filipendula rubra* 'Venusta' contrast with the drooping semi-transparent spires of a tall *Sanguisorba* (possibly *S.* 'Korean Snow').

Table 2 Spires and plumes for seasonal interest

Plant	Form	Seasonal interest
Digitalis ferruginea	Spire Seedheads	Unusual rusty-orange vertical accents. Good for dotting through other planting.
Calamagrostis brachytricha	Plume Seedheads	Dead flower heads last through the winter. Looks lovely backlit in low sun.
Astilbe chinensis 'Vision in White'	Plume Dying flower heads	Produces masses of flowers. The dead brown flower heads last into the autumn.
Veronica spicata 'Royal Candles'	Spire Dying flower heads	Dramatic purple flowers through the summer. The low-growing foliage is a good ground cover.

Bobbles and spheres

Spheres can add formality to a design and are often used as repeated accents amongst lower-growing perennials. Bobbles are smaller than spheres, occurring in groups, standing out as intense dots of colour against softer flower forms or a green background.

The bobbles of the dying flower heads of Phlomis echo the spheres of *Allium* and the smaller bobbles of *Cirsium rivulare* 'Atropurpureum' in the background to unify this planting scheme designed by the author. (With special thanks to the Provost and Fellows of The Queen's College.)

Table 3 Bobbles and spheres for seasonal interest

Plant	Form	Seasonal interest
Knautia macedonica	Bobble Semi-transparent	Free flowering over a long period.
Phlomis russeliana	Bobble Seedheads	Flowers for a long period over the summer and the dead flower heads on strong stems persist into the winter. Often keeps its leaves through the winter.
Echinops ritro	Sphere Seedheads	Interesting prickly silver/blue foliage and spherical flower heads late in the summer. These last well into the autumn.
Astrantia major	Bobble	Long flowering period. The leaves can be cut back and will regrow forming a clump of green ground cover later in the summer and autumn. Comes into leaf early.
Cirsium rivulare 'Atropurpureum'	Bobble	Attractive purple flowers held above divided leaves. Continues to have a presence into the autumn.
Agapanthus 'Morning Star'	Sphere Seedheads	Dramatic blue spheres above strappy foliage. Seedheads last into the winter. Good in pots.

Dying flowers and seedheads

For the seasonal garden, it is worth having a selection of flowers that die in an attractive manner or have long-lasting seedheads. Umbellifers lend structure and a sense of calm to naturalistic planting schemes, the horizontality of the flower heads contrasting well with the fragility of vertical grasses. Many become more dramatic in the winter – their stiff, branched stems and dried seedheads are a striking presence for many months. Open daisy-like flowers can also have an interesting and persistent winter form. Their petals die to leave only the centre of the flower head – a little brown bobble.

The seedheads of some spires last well into the winter retaining their vertical forms, and plumes may also persist but their form changes and becomes less interesting as the plant dies. The exceptions are the late-flowering grasses with their strong upright flower heads.

Open daisy-like flowers of *Aster* x *frikartii* 'Monch' contrast with the semi-transparent screen of the plumes of *Calamagrostis brachytricha*, designed by the author. (With special thanks to the Provost and Fellows of The Queen's College.)

Dying flower heads of *Leucanthemum vulgare*.

Table 4 Dying flowers and seedheads for seasonal interest

Plant	Form	Seasonal interest
Cenolophium denudatum	Umbellifer Seedheads	Dramatic tall flower stems above a mound of finely divided leaves.
Rudbeckia laciniata 'Herbstsonne'	Open/daisy-like Dying flower heads	Flowers for a long period later in the summer bringing interest to the back of a border. The central buttons can last well into the winter.
Leucanthemum vulgare	Open/daisy-like Dying flower heads	Produces a mass of white flowers in early summer that die prettily leaving little brown buttons for a few more weeks before needing to be cut back. Good in flowering lawns.
Aster × *frikartii* 'Monch'	Open/daisy-like Dying flower heads	The leaves are late appearing in spring but this aster flowers for many weeks and can persist after the flowers have died before needing to be cut back. Copes with drought.
Achillea 'Cloth of Gold'	Flat-headed Dying flower heads	The dead flower heads remain standing for months and even survive frost and snow. Copes well with drought.
Hylotelephium 'Red Cauli'	Flat-headed Dying flower heads	The new grey-green growth is attractive early in the summer and the flowers persist for many weeks. Eventually the dead flower heads topple over but they can remain throughout the winter.

Semi-transparent screens

Semi-transparent perennials and grasses are valuable in any planting scheme and even more so when designing for seasonal succession, the persistence of their dead flower and seedheads giving interest when other plants have died back. A bonus is how these delicate plants with their open see-through structure move with the slightest breeze, creating a mysterious and romantic atmosphere in the garden. These screens are useful when designing successional schemes as they can be placed to add height to the front of the border, catching the eye when other plants behind are fading or are not yet in bloom. Or they can be rippled and dotted through static clusters of perennials and contrasted with more formal clipped shapes. Some take up very little space and so lend themselves to planting through and amongst clusters of other plants. In the table below you will see some of these species taking the form of dotty screens: they could also be included as examples in the next section.

The long-flowering *Verbena bonariensis* in front of a dramatically coloured rendered wall.

Sanguisorba and *Miscanthus* at Bury Court designed by Christopher Bradley-Hole. The dead flower heads of the grass will last through the winter.

Table 5 Screens for seasonal interest

Plant	Form	Seasonal interest
Oenothera lindheimeri ssp. (formally *Gaura*)	Screen	Delicate pink and white flowers for four months over the summer.
Molinia 'Transparent'	Screen Seedheads	A dramatic tall grass with semi-transparent flower heads that rise to 1.8m above strap-like foliage creating a muted, hazy glow through which to view brighter neighbours. Seedheads last into the winter.
Foeniculum vulgare 'Smokey'	Screen Seedheads	Feathery bronze foliage and statuesque flower heads that last through the winter creating sculptural forms. Happily self-seeds.
Deschampsia cespitosa 'Bronzeschleier'	Screen Seedheads	A graceful airy grass with small silvery flowers that turn golden brown as they age and last into the autumn.
Panicum virgatum 'Rehbraun'	Screen Seedheads	Deep green leaves turn bright red in late summer. Flowers are also a reddish brown.
Sanguisorba officinalis 'Tanna'	Dotty screen Seedheads	A lower growing variety with red button-like flowers held above finely cut green leaves.
Thalictrum delavayi	Dotty screen	Delicate purple flowers above attractive grey-green leaves. Stands well into the autumn and takes up very little space amongst other plants. There is also a white variety.

Dots and carpets

Less assuming flowers can make their presence felt through their sheer quantity: the individual flowers may be less exciting but *en masse* they play a part in the design, forming carpets of colour. These species can also be dotted through other planting, standing out against a background of green foliage. When using these perennials in a successional scheme, the designer usually must think about introducing additional species to extend the flowering season as most of these smaller flower heads do not last into the winter months.

Thalictrum delavayi is useful as a dotty screen and to wind through more static planting.

Origanum laevigatum 'Herrenhausen' intermingles with a sedum and a trailing *Clematis* 'Polish Spirit'.

Table 6 Dots and carpets for seasonal interest

Plant	Form	Seasonal interest
Geranium renardii	Carpet	Flowers through the summer. The unusual sage-green leaves last well into the autumn.
Dianthus carthusianorum	Dots	A tall variety with single flowers above grassy green foliage. Flowers all through the summer. Can be used in meadows.
Heuchera 'Lime Marmalade'	Dots and carpet	Bushy ground cover that brings a touch of lime green brightness to shady places throughout the year. The delicate white flowers form a semi-transparent screen above the leaves in summer.
Primula vulgaris	Carpet	Primroses flower for several months in winter and early spring bringing delicate colour and a lovely scent. The leaves do not mind being shaded later in the year.
Symphyotrichum lateriflorum var. *horizontalis*	Carpet Dying flower heads	Low-growing, pink-flowered ground cover. Dead flower heads last throughout the winter. Cut back in early March.
Nepeta racemosa 'Walker's Low'	Carpet	Crinkly grey leaves form mounds above which rise dark stems and buds. Flowers throughout the summer and leaves last through the winter.
Origanum laevigatum 'Herrenhausen'	Carpet	Shrubby stems with tiny leaves form dense mats. Purple flowers on stiff stems last through the summer and into the autumn and are loved by bees. New leaves start to appear in late winter/early spring and look good interspersed with snowdrops.

Scent

The scent of a flower and the aromatic qualities of leaves are a bonus for visitors to the garden. Site these plants near paths or around a door to ensure that they can be fully appreciated when pausing to enjoy the aroma, or when brushing past to release the fragrance. Night-scented flowers can be a delight, especially when placed near a seating area or by the French doors. Scented shrubs are especially useful when designing for seasonal succession as many flower in the winter months: examples that also have evergreen leaves include, *Mahonia × media* 'Charity', *Sarcococca confusa* and *Elaeagnus × ebbingei*. In a large garden with space for different species to provide interest in the other seasons of the year, *Viburnum × bodnantense* 'Dawn', *Chimonanthus praecox*, known as wintersweet, and *Lonicera fragrantissima*, winter-flowering honeysuckle, can be planted for their gloriously scented blossoms in January and February.

Many climbers are scented and are best placed near a path or bench or on a pergola so we can enjoy getting up close to fully experience the aroma. Examples include the evergreen *Clematis armandii* 'Apple Blossom', *Wisteria* ssp., a range of roses in different colours, honeysuckle, *Trachelospermum jasminoides* and *Akebia quinata* with its unusual, tiny, maroon-chocolate coloured flowers early in the year that smell almost of spicy vanilla.

Leaf Shape and Texture

Flowers may be the first thing we think about when choosing plants but, as they are usually transient features of the garden, it pays to consider leaf shape and texture. Large, bold-leaved plants draw attention and hold their own when contrasted with hard landscaping elements – patios, paths, rocks and water. In contrast, smaller leaved species fade into the background where they can be a foil to other more dramatic plants, or

The textural grey-green leaves and lime coloured flower heads of *Euphorbia characias* subsp. *wulfenii* complement those of the *Macleaya* in this small, shady urban garden designed by the author.

Textures of green enliven a shady town garden in London designed by the author.

create a framework to show off a riotous display of colour in a particular season of the year. Repeating an unusual leaf shape, be it large or small, unifies a design and creates a sense of rhythm as you move around the garden. Many evergreen small-leafed plants can be clipped into spheres, pyramids or blocks and placed among more informal plants to add a static resting place for the eye. These punctuation plants look good when repeated around the garden and give interest throughout the year.

A personal favourite for repetition in semi-shade is the humble *Epimedium*; the heart-shaped leaves unfurl, often in a delicate bronze shade, just as the tiny flowers are coming into full bloom. Depending on the variety (there are many to choose from), the leaves turn to green with some bronze markings, growing bigger and forming a dense ground cover during the summer and persisting until the following February when they are cut back to reveal the curled new flower shoots.

Leaf texture is part of the attraction of many species: glaucous *Euphorbia characias*, furry silver *Stachys byzantina*, rough grey culinary sage, sharply cut *Cynara cardunculus*, feathery *Euphorbia cyparissias* and finely cut *Sambucus nigra* 'Black Lace'. Some larger-leafed plants provide months of interest as leaves unfurl and sometimes change colour through the seasons. One example is the chartreuse foliage of *Hosta* 'Great Expectations' that contrasts with a yellow centre which deepens in colour over the summer and then turns creamy yellow and white in the autumn.

Ferns are especially useful when thinking about leaf texture and year-round interest. The bronze, curled new growth is compelling, then the fronds gradually unfurl to become significant green forms in the garden with leaf texture ranging from the slightly crinkled, strap-like *Asplenium scolopendrium* to the complicated cut forms of the *Polystichum* ssp., the feathery *Matteuccia struthiopteris* and the unusual divided leaves of the native *Polypodium cambricum* 'Oakleyae'.

The Challenges of Small Spaces

Many designers working in towns and cities are primarily designing small gardens. These bring their own challenges. The client often has expectations about what they want to include in the garden and there is the need to explain what is possible in such a confined space. The light levels may be low or reduced considerably in winter, when surrounding houses block out the sun. In new-build houses the soils will be depleted and often include rubble and waste left by the developers. Front gardens sometimes double as bin and bike storage spaces and often as a car park. New extensions with floor-to-ceiling glass look out over the garden in all seasons. And most people would often like to have a lawn and colour all the year round.

In these cases, it is tempting to focus on pruned evergreen shrubs to give low maintenance interest. Box, yew and bay are easily clipped to shapes that stand out against their surroundings. Alternatives to these include *Ilex crenata* with tiny, glossy leaves that is a good substitute for box, which is now under threat from the box tree caterpillar. *Viburnum tinus*, *Sarcococca ruscifolia* and *S. confusa* can also be clipped – all have white flowers in winter and the *Sarcococca* is beautifully scented. Also scented is *Daphne* × *transatlantica* 'Eternal Fragrance' that has white flowers throughout the spring and summer and *D. odora* 'Aureomarginata' with leaves edged in gold and flowering in spring. *Pittosporum* ssp., with their range of leaf colours and variegations are also useful; they can be pruned to different sizes and shapes depending on the space allotted. A slightly different variety is the low-growing *Pittosporum tobira* 'Nanum' with larger glossy leaves and scented white flowers in spring. It forms a low mound of foliage that looks especially effective contrasted with grasses or hostas and ferns in gravel gardens and in combination with the lighter green, feathery *Acer palmatum* 'Dissectum' it can bring a hint of the Japanese garden to a planting scheme. For a Mediterranean-style garden in sun, *Olea europaea* is a silver-leafed small tree that can be pruned to a 'lollipop' shape. Other silver-leafed species such as lavender can be planted around the olive, but I prefer to avoid too much grey and to create contrasts with herbs such as a prostrate rosemary and flowering thyme and marjoram or to select one of the varieties of French lavender. This combination for a sunny site can be adapted to planting in pots on a patio or balcony where space is limited.

However, it is not necessary, nor indeed desirable, to merely rely on evergreens and it is possible to design planting to change with the seasons, even in small spaces. Start by ensuring that at least one bed is deep enough to layer different species; if this is in the sun all the better, but there is also plenty of choice for a bed in semi-shade. Designing on a diagonal can be an interesting way of introducing larger beds in a small space. Doing away with a lawn leaves spaces for a bench or small table surrounded by dense planting. Or a more open gravel area can be designed to show off grasses and accent plants with long-lasting seedheads.

Ensure all the walls and fences are put to use to support and display a range of climbers and wall plants, but remember these need space to expand away from the wall and will take up some of the valuable depth of a bed. Wall shrubs that are pruned and tied in to a framework are useful when space is at a premium. Examples are *Chaenomeles speciosa* 'Geisha Girl' with salmon pink flowers and *C.* × *superba* 'Pink Lady', both flowering from late winter into spring and developing quince-like fruits. Another unusual spring-flowering wall shrub is *Ribes speciosum*, which has droplets of scarlet fuchsia-like flowers.

Deciduous shrubs do not look their best in the winter, unless they have coloured stems, and if included in a small garden they should be sited where they are not so visible from the window: perhaps it is best to choose deciduous wall shrubs rather than using them in a small bed. However, the bare branches of multi-stem shrubs and small trees can create eye-catching sculptural forms and allow for planting beneath to extend the seasons of interest. An *Amelanchier* is an obvious choice, but you could also lift the crown on *Osmanthus* × *burkwoodii* by keeping the vertical stems and removing any side shoots. Trees with interesting bark also make good multi-stem focal points: *Betula nigra* has shaggy, peeling copper-brown bark and *Arbutus unedo* combines peeling brown bark with white flowers and strawberry-like fruits. A pretty winter combination can be created by placing *Betula utilis* var. *jacquemontii* behind *Viburnum* × *bodnantense* 'Dawn'. The bright white trunk of the Himalayan birch is a wonderful foil to the soft pink flowers of the *Viburnum*. If you want to choose a native tree, *Corylus avellana* can be kept in check by coppicing, creating an interesting form and with the bonus of catkins in winter. You will discover more about trees and shrubs for winter interest in Chapter 5 and coppicing in Chapter 3. Although there may only be room for two or three species, these shrubs and trees form the bones of the garden around which flow the perennials, grasses and bulbs.

Finally, if a lawn is non-negotiable, plant it with crocuses, snowdrops and small early-flowering narcissus: two good choices are *Narcissus assoanus* with its short leaves and scented yellow blooms and *N.* 'Hawera', which has delicate clusters of starry lemon-yellow flowers. The crocuses and snowdrops can be allowed to self-seed in the lawn, but the dead flower heads of the narcissus should be removed.

This courtyard is part of the larger garden designed by Frederick Gibberd, but it demonstrates how different forms can be used to balance a design and create harmony in even the smallest of spaces.

Two Small Beds in Semi-Shade

Many small town gardens are surrounded by buildings or shaded by overhanging shrubs and trees, resulting in beds that are often both shaded and dry. The annotated photo shown here, of a tiny front garden on heavy clay, facing northeast, demonstrates what can be achieved in even the smallest of spaces. The interlacing planting is almost self-sufficient requiring no watering and little maintenance, except for occasional cutting back and pruning of the shrubs and weeding of the path. The native woodruff, *Galium odoratum* is a useful ground cover that will easily take over a bed, so should be used with care. The other plants seem to cope with the competition.

The second example is of a bed in a back garden facing south, again on clay. The diagonal design has ensured there is space for a slightly larger bed in this narrow garden. There is little that is evergreen in this scheme except for some ferns and *Epimedium*. Instead there is a reliance on bulbs, autumn colour and the form of the multi-stemmed *Amelanchier* to provide seasonal interest. As can be seen in the photos this does mean that there is a period over winter where browns

A small shady front garden photographed in April. A The form and red berries of *Cotoneaster horizontalis* add interest in winter. B Arum brings drama in winter and spring. C *Milium effusum* 'Aureum' self-seeds giving dots of brightness. D Chaenomeles has been flowering since December. E *Helleborus foetidus* self-seeds. F Polypodium battles with the mass of vegetation to give year-round interest. G A little self-seeding is allowed in the path. H *Helleborus orientalis* has finished flowering and the leaves now add texture. It is allowed to self-seed. I *Galium odoratum* colonises all available space. It dies back in winter but is now showing bright green new growth and will soon be covered with white flowers. J *Dicentra spectabilis* rises dramatically from the ground cover to give a few weeks of colour before disappearing. K The early leaves of *Geranium* 'Ann Folkard'. Its dots of magenta-pink will scramble over other plants throughout the summer. L Grape hyacinths and bluebells emerge after the early narcissus has died back. Later, *Sedum* and *Heuchera* will fill this space.

are the predominant colour; introducing a bright evergreen ground cover such as *Euonymus* 'Emerald Gaiety' or planting *Trachelospermum jasminoides* along the fence would enhance this dormant period.

Nevertheless, there is colour over a long period from early snowdrops through a range of bulbs, *Pulmonaria*, *Epimedium* and blossom and then long-flowering *Geranium* and *Astrantia*, followed by Japanese anemones and

Veronicastrum. *Hydrangea quercifolia* provides year-round interest, forming a shrubby mound with large deeply lobed leaves that turn reddish purple in autumn and last into the following spring. The bark is brown and peeling and the dense, conical flowers start as white and become edged with pink. Like the *Amelanchier*, the form of this shrub also allows for some planting beneath, where light penetrates.

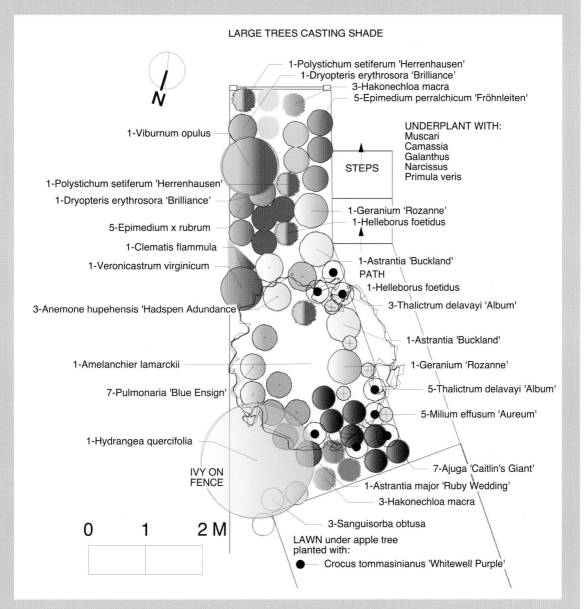

Plan for a small bed designed on the diagonal with a path running along the side.

A selection of images from different times of the year. Clockwise from top left: *Hydrangea quercifolia* and *Amelanchier*; *Epimedium*; *Hydrangea quercifolia* and *Hakonechloa*; *Hydrangea quercifolia* and *Amelanchier*; *Amelanchier*.

The same bed in July – dots of the long-flowering *Geranium* and *Astrantia* provide colour and the spires of *Veronicastrum* are beginning to form before the pinks of the *Anemone* 'Hadspen Abundance' take over.

CHAPTER 3

WARP AND WEFT APPROACH

Whether you are starting to design a garden from scratch or revamping existing beds, creating a planting plan is a helpful way to take a step back and think about how the garden will evolve and grow with time. Often it is tempting to walk around a garden centre or nursery selecting beautiful flowering plants that catch your eye, but it is important to consider how plants work together and how they contribute to the overall design. Of course, once on the ground and setting out the pots, changes are made and decisions reconsidered. As Christopher Lloyd once wrote 'I would always prefer to make up my mind on the spot about how to do my weaving ... We want to know which plants we'd like to see near to one another before starting ... and have them ready at hand, but after that a measure of ad-lib-bing will give us a sense of exhilaration' (Lloyd, 2004).

In the next chapter, I will discuss the many ways of drawing up a plan – it might only consist of indicative placings and lists or percentages of different species. In this chapter we will look at one way of thinking about planting design that I call the 'warp and weft' approach. My colleague, Alex Johnson, and I, first introduced this conceptual approach in our book *Habitat Creation in Garden Design* (2022). When designing with plants we are creating a sculptural three-dimensional mass that

changes both horizontally and vertically: it expands upwards to the light; it flops to the ground; it keels over; it stretches in unexpected directions; it even disappears completely. A planting design always has its challenges, but if we embrace the changes with the seasons and take pleasure in even the brown and dead vegetation, we can always find enjoyment. This is the delight of gardening – each month there will be something new to excite.

Using the concept of weaving allows for these changes whilst also giving a fluid way to think about design. In weaving cloth, the warp consists of the threads that are strung lengthwise between a frame and are held stationary under tension. The weft weaves back and forth through these warp threads. Because the warp is forming the bones of the cloth the threads need to be strong, but the weft can be made of finer and more ornate fibres. You can begin to see how this concept might be applied to gardens.

Throughout this chapter you will see the concept of warp and weft illustrated in a large courtyard garden at an Oxford college in the south of England. The garden is surrounded by tall walls and the beds were already laid out when I undertook this project. There were also three mature trees on site – a magnolia, an evergreen

(With special thanks to the Provost and Fellows of The Queen's College.)

oak and a bay. Extensive work had been undertaken and part of the brief was to create privacy and screen a new access route along the east side of the garden. The garden is designed to attract birds and insects and the client asked for plenty of colour, drama and excitement at different times of the year. It is also a place for relaxation, entertaining, has to accommodate large groups of people and is viewed from all sides, and from high windows, throughout the year. It benefits from an informed team of gardeners and thus maintenance is not an issue. The soil is good quality with plenty of organic matter and fairly well-drained, although under the evergreen oak it is extremely dry.

The Bones of the Garden

Before discussing the warp and weft approach in detail it is worth taking an overall look at trees and shrubs; they form the bones of any garden and are the structural points around which other planting weaves. In a garden for seasonal succession, they must be chosen carefully as they should add something to the scene throughout the year. Even in winter when the individual bare branches of shrubs may seem to be devoid of interest, there are details to catch the attention: sculptural gnarled branches standing out against the sky; textures of bark to run the hand across; fissures and cracks to give character; coloured stems and twigs shining in low sunlight; buds gradually swelling and breaking; catkins hanging from bare brown branches.

Apart from the individual attributes of colour, texture and habit, there are also long-term implications to consider when choosing a tree or shrub:

- The time taken to reach maturity
- Their longevity
- Their ultimate size
- Whether they can be pruned
- How they should be rejuvenated if necessary
- How the balance of mass and void is affected through the years.

The fascinating shapes of the branches of this small tree in a garden in Japan are enhanced by the reflective properties of the water below (© Rosemary Lee).

However, when choosing trees, the most important factor to consider is the climate crisis. Trees can help with the challenges that we face, especially in our cities where they can mitigate the heat island effect, help regulate storm water run-off and play a part in carbon sequestration (Segall, 2022). They also have cultural and health benefits and provide habitats for wildlife. Again, I return to the importance of species diversity. This means that choosing a native species is not always the answer; a mix of native and non-natives is more likely to result in a long-term resilient planting scheme.

The list that follows contains a few suggestions of trees and shrubs that may be able to cope more successfully with changes to the climate and that are useful in a seasonal successional garden.

An olive grove in Crete. The ancient forms of the trees contrast with the delicate ground cover beneath (© Sergio Denche).

Table 7 Trees and shrubs to use in a successional scheme

Tree/shrub	Attributes for seasonal succession	Comments
Crataegus persimilis 'Prunifolia'	White spring flowers and dramatic red and orange autumn colour.	Copes with hot, dry conditions (RHS, n.d.-h).
Euonymus alatus	Fiery crimson autumn colour with reddish-purple fruits split to reveal orange seed capsules. The bare stems reveal their strange corky wings.	This makes a spreading bush of about 2 × 2.5m in twenty years. Tolerates most soils and sun or part shade.
Juniperus scopulorum 'Skyrocket'	Narrow, columnar evergreen with blue-green foliage.	Copes with hot, dry conditions (RHS, n.d.-h) and may be better able to cope with a changing climate.
Koelreuteria paniculata	Yellow flowers in summer and yellow leaf colour in autumn. Good for pollinators. Interesting seed pods last through the winter.	Raise the canopy and prune to create a sculptural form in a small garden. May be useful in changing climate, tolerates cold winters and long hot summers (Willaert, n.d.) (Segall, 2022).
Lyonothamnus floribundus subsp. *Asplenifolius*	This evergreen tree has fern-like leaves and a peeling red-brown bark. Small white flowers in spring and summer.	Sculptural form is useful in urban and courtyard gardens. Combines well with Mediterranean plants. May be useful in changing climate as it is tolerant of different conditions, but it does not like to be in wet soil. Only lives to around 35 years (Architectural Plants, n.d.).

Table 7 *(Cont'd)*

Tree/shrub	Attributes for seasonal succession	Comments
Morus nigra	Horizontal, ancient looking branches, edible dark berries, yellow leaves in autumn.	Mulberries are long-lived and can even be grown in pots for a long period. If there is space, they make an attractive feature in a lawn and they can also be trained against a wall.
Osmanthus × burkwoodii	Dark green evergreen leaves and highly scented white flowers in spring.	Fairly slow growing. Copes with sun and shade. Raise the crown on this shrub to form a small multi-stem tree and plant shade-loving ground cover beneath.
Parrotia persica 'Vanessa'	Leaves emerge bronze and burgundy turning green in summer and then shades of bronze, crimson, orange and gold. Small spider-like red flowers on bare stems in winter and early spring.	A more upright form of the Persian Ironwood. Tolerant of air pollution (Willaert, n.d.). Fairly slow growing. Autumn colour is better on acid soils.
Prunus padus 'Colorata'	Racemes of pale pink flowers in spring followed by small black fruits. Young leaves are deep purple red.	Tolerant of waterlogged soils (RHS, n.d.-h). A good tree for pollinators and birds.
Pyrus calleryana 'Chanticleer'	A medium-sized tree with early spring blossom and autumn colour.	Copes with hot, dry conditions (RHS, n.d.-h).
Taxus baccata	Evergreen leaves, unusual tiny clusters of male flowers in spring, red berries that are attractive to birds. The fastigiate form makes a good focal point.	Native to the UK. Can be used in topiary and as a hedge and can also be pruned back hard into the old wood to rejuvenate. After pruning feed and water.

A tapestry of forms and textures beneath *Koelreuteria paniculata* framed by a clipped hedge in Beth Chatto's gravel garden.

Creating the Warp

There is, of course, a wonderful selection of trees and shrubs to choose from, even when restricting yourself to those with several seasons of interest. This is the planting that creates a long-lasting structure – the warp – and it is usually the first thing designers think about when drawing up a planting plan. Before starting on the plan itself, compile a list of possible plants – a palette for the design. Often students are told to produce this list and then to halve the number of species chosen to ensure that the principles of unity and simplicity are adhered to. However, as I have suggested, diversity is important for seasonal succession, sustainability and enhancing biodiversity: therefore, keep the list long for the moment.

Plants chosen for the warp can be divided into three categories depending on their function in the design: anchors, frames and punctuation.

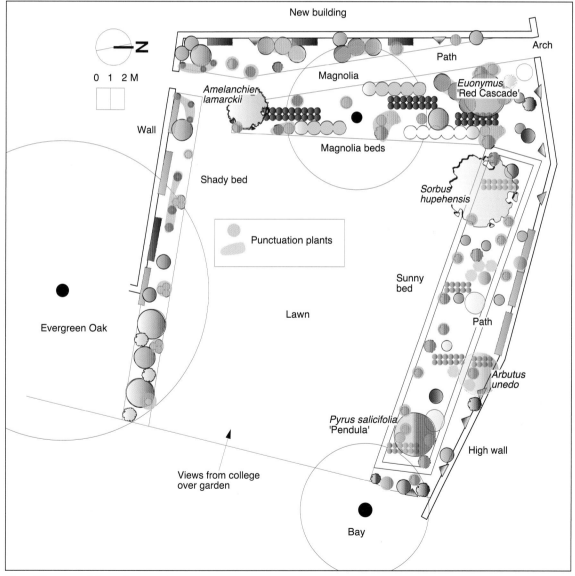

Plan of the warp at the college garden.

Anchors

Anchoring plants create the main structure of a garden. They can be thought of as static features around which the perennials and grasses flow. Shrubs and trees make good anchoring plants; the most obvious ones are the rounded evergreens that are periodically clipped to maintain their form. When thinking about the different seasons, these are an easy choice. Habit, form and texture can also create interest, as can the colours of bark, leaves, berries and flowers. In certain cases, a tall grass such as *Miscanthus* can be used as an anchoring plant. Anchors may be designed as focal points and it may be desirable to purchase a specimen plant, even though it will probably sulk for a few years after it is planted and not put on much more growth for a while.

In the college garden, the mature magnolia and the evergreen oak already fulfil the role of anchoring plants. Indeed, the oak dominates the neighbouring courtyard and casts heavy, dry shade. The magnolia is a spreading, pyramidal shape and contributes to the screening of the new access path. Because of its size and form it became a ready-made focal point in the design, attracting the attention from across the large area of lawn. However, magnolia is not a tree I would necessarily choose for varied seasonal interest: it is wonderful in bud and bloom but then relies on its form to provide interest. In this design I ensured that the surrounding planting attracted attention at other times of the year.

New anchors consisted of five trees. Multi-stemmed *Amelanchier lamarckii*, with its distinctive form, bronze new growth and creamy-white blossom as well as the bright late-summer berries and leaf colour, and *Euonymus* 'Red Cascade' with its unusual fruits and vivid autumn colour, are sited to screen the new path. The evergreen *Arbutus unedo* has interesting bark, contrasting with the beautiful old wall, and red-orange fruits that are often present at the same time as the white flowers. *Sorbus hupehensis* has pinnate grey-green leaves, white spring flowers and glorious autumn colour as well as pink-tinged, white berries. And finally, *Pyrus salicifolia* 'Pendula' that relies on its weeping habit together with its silvery leaves to give interest.

Evergreen anchors include *Choisya* 'Aztec Pearl', which has white spring flowers, varieties of *Pittosporum* and *Sarcococca*, all of which are repeated around the garden creating a rhythm to the planting. There are also the deciduous *Cotinus* 'Grace' with wonderful autumn colours and the deep purple foliage and pink catkins of *Corylus avellana* 'Zellernuss'.

The shapes of the branches of this magnolia at Myddleton House in North London create interest through the year.

Frames

Framing plants bring structure to more ephemeral and less ordered planting. They can be designed to contrast with a winding sweep of perennials and grasses or to provide a backdrop for more showy, flamboyant plants. They could frame a focal point and in a seasonal garden, if the accent plant dies back in winter, they can provide interest before fading into the background again with the new growth of spring.

Frames also double as screening plants; in the college garden the view of the magnolia bed is of blocks of yew hedging (kept clipped to heights of 1.2m–1.8m) and in the summer and autumn these contrast with layers of the flowering grass, *Calamagrostis brachytricha*.

Clipped *Buxus* and *Taxus* hedging and trained clipped *Pyracantha*, with red berries, create a theme which runs through the garden much like a musical refrain repeated in a variety of forms. The horizontality of the clipped hedges echoes the horizontal wooden slats, which are a striking element of the new building. More than a decade on, it is worth noting that because of the problems with box caterpillar, I would now not choose to plant box so extensively in a garden. Alternatives include *Ilex crenata*, *Sarcococca* ssp., *Taxus baccata* 'Repandens' and *Pittosporum* 'Golf Ball'.

Climbers and wall shrubs can also be used as frames. A scented wisteria is trained over the arch at the entrance to the garden framing the path and the view. On the old, high wall are three fan-trained apples, chosen from a selection of traditional varieties. The fan shape is echoed on the opposite wall between the two courtyards, in the training of the scented evergreen wall shrub, *Osmanthus delavayi* and a pink-flowered *Chaenomeles*. The wall and the trained trees and shrubs are in effect reciprocal frames, each showing off the other to best advantage. On the plan these frames are shown as blocks of green to emphasise their clipped and trained forms.

Clipped blocks of yew are used as frames behind *Calamagrostis brachytricha*. (With special thanks to the Provost and Fellows of The Queen's College.)

Cues to Care

More than three decades ago landscape architect and academic, Joan Iverson Nassauer (1995) outlined the importance of including what she calls 'cues to care' in designed landscapes. Nassauer was discussing ways of framing ecosystems to give a cultural context to the processes that were taking place and to indicate that the landscape was cared for. The idea of creating an orderly frame around something that could be seen as disordered can also be applied to designed landscapes and gardens. This may be as simple as mowing a strip of grass along the edge of a path or through a wildflower meadow.

In the warp and weft system, framing plants can be used as cues to care. They not only indicate a level of care, but also help to make the landscape more understandable and acceptable. This is particularly relevant when thinking about successional gardens in the winter months when they may not be looking at their best. Questions may be asked about why dead and dying leaves and seedheads are left, seemingly just to collapse and rot. Attractive evergreens and species with bright berries or stems can be placed to frame the views or highlight focal points and take attention away from the more mundane areas of the garden in winter. Similarly, punctuation plants that retain a winter presence can lead the eye around the space, passing over the dead vegetation, but also letting you know that the garden is still cared for.

A meadow contained by the frames of pleached trees at The Old Vicarage, East Ruston.

Punctuation

The third element in the warp is the punctuation. Individual plants or groupings, repeated around the garden, act as full stops or commas, creating a breathing space where the bustle and drama of the rippling perennial mosaic comes to a rest for a moment. Their repetition brings a rhythm to the design and a sense of unity. In a small garden these groups might be repeated three or four times, but in a larger space different cultivars of the same species could be used to give greater variety while still maintaining the sense of rhythm.

Plants with a strong rounded or domed shape make good punctuation. They may have interesting textured or variegated foliage, or perhaps red stems in winter. Flowers are a bonus as long as they are not too showy. It is important that punctuation plants provide a restful pause for the eye.

In the college courtyard, punctuation plants include several varieties of *Hebe*, creating low evergreen hummocks with purple or white flowers at different times of the year. In places, *Hebe* 'Mrs Winder' is planted with *Pittosporum tobira* 'Nanum' and *Acer palmatum* 'Dissectum', creating mounds of dark, narrow leaves that contrast with the feathery, bright greens of the *Acer* and the larger, glossy leaves of the *Pittosporum*. In the shady bed, *Asplenium scolopendrium*, either singly or in groups of three, punctuates the front of the border. Also in this bed between the two courtyards, three fastigiate yews give height and drama to the mainly low planting in front of the wall. Clipped box balls occur in all the beds – an evergreen rounded presence throughout the year. In the magnolia beds large groups of *Cornus sanguinea* 'Midwinter Fire' punctuate the lower growing perennials. In summer it forms an unobtrusive frame, coming into its own as punctuation in the winter months when its bright red stems echo the berries of the *Pyracantha*. More *Hebes* are repeated along the sunny bed and here *Euphorbia characias* subsp. *wulfenii* also adds a dramatic punctuation to the riot of colour. The punctuation plants shown on the plan are shaded in pale brown to give an idea of how often they occur and their positions.

The rounded forms of *Pittosporum* and *Hebe* create punctuation in the warp in front of the low frame of *Buxus*.
(With special thanks to the Provost and Fellows of The Queen's College.)

Frames and punctuation along the long sunny border. (With special thanks to the Provost and Fellows of The Queen's College.)

A view of the planting along the path with the anchoring tree, *Euonymus* 'Red Cascade'. (With special thanks to the Provost and Fellows of The Queen's College.)

Adding the Weft

Once the plants in the warp are drawn in approximate positions on the plan, the weft can be interwoven between them in sweeps, swirls, waves, dots and groups. There are four different ways in which this can be done: rippling, clustering, interlacing and chance. It is unlikely that you will use all four techniques in one design; however, combining several techniques can lead to an increased diversity and more opportunities for seasonal interest.

In the college garden I use two of the techniques – clusters and ripples – to introduce perennials and grasses that weave around the repeated elements in the warp, giving colour and drama which change with the seasons. There are vertical deep pink spires of *Veronicastrum*, pink, lilac and white daisy-like flower heads of *Echinacea* and *Aster* and yellow pompoms of the *Phlomis*. The grasses, *Calamagrostis* and *Deschampsia* create semi-transparent screens, moving with the wind; the seedheads remain for much of the winter, as do the flower heads of some of the

Plan of the weft at the college garden showing the ripples and clusters.

perennials. In spring a succession of bulbs provides colour and an element of surprise and anticipation. Most dramatic are the *Nectaroscordum* with nodding buff-coloured flowers and the deep blue *Camassia*. Under the coppiced, purple-leafed hazel, *Corylus avellana* 'Zellernuss', are evergreen ferns and hellebores, creating a woodland feel to this section of the garden in deep shade under the evergreen oak.

Clustering

I discuss using clusters first because this closely approximates to traditional techniques for creating planting plans. If you want a more formal or ordered garden, then this is the technique to use. Small gardens, where long sweeps of plants are not appropriate, also benefit from this approach. Grouping plants into clusters of the same species gives impact, especially when in flower. The garden resembles a colourful tapestry of separate blocks of colour. Each block remains fairly distinct, contrasting with its neighbour in form, colour and flowering period. Clusters are repeated around the garden to give continuity and to lead the eye around, drawing you into the planting. Good examples of using clusters can be seen in the designs of Piet Oudolf, although he is working on a large scale with big groups of one species. In smaller spaces the effect is not so dramatic.

For a more informal atmosphere to the garden, it is possible to add a random element to the weft by dotting semi-transparent species and bulbs through the clusters. Allowing self-seeding of these ephemeral plants leads to a wilder aesthetic, but can also make maintenance more difficult.

There is much discussion and conflicting advice on the spacing to allow between plants when creating a planting plan. A balance needs to be drawn between the desire for immediate impact and the long-term health of the plants. Perennials and grasses grown close together in a mixed matrix are more likely to be self-supporting, each plant twining and clambering around its neighbour. However, plants that are overcrowded and competing for nutrients may not thrive and may need to be lifted and moved after a couple of years. Nurseries often recommend planting seven or nine perennials per square metre, which can seem excessive and is also expensive. However, leaving bare earth is not a sustainable way of gardening; this is where annuals or short-lived perennials can be useful, including those that seed themselves around, as you will discover in Chapter 4. The plans in this book tend to show larger shrubs as 1–1.5m circles and perennials and grasses with spacings of 40, 50 or 60cm.

There are plants that particularly lend themselves to being designed in clusters – they look good *en masse*. Those with flat and open flower heads such as asters, daisies and umbellifers make a striking display when in bloom. Good examples for the successional garden are *Aster* × *frikartti* 'Monch', *Echinacea* ssp. and *Rudbeckia* 'Goldsturm'. Then there are species with smaller flowers that could get lost in a sea of green if they are not planted in groups – smaller flowering daisies, the lower-growing *Sanguisorba officinalis* 'Tanna', *Heuchera* ssp. and smaller scabious-like

Hydrangea 'Annabelle' and *Euphorbia* are planted in clusters with ripples of the semi-transparent grass *Calamagrostis brachytricha* running though the foreground. (With special thanks to the Provost and Fellows of The Queen's College.)

Clusters of *Echinacea* and *Aster* in front of a low frame of *Buxus* with ripples of *Calamagrostis* x *acutiflora* 'Karl Foerster' behind. (With special thanks to the Provost and Fellows of The Queen's College.)

flowers such as *Knautia macedonica*. Other perennials that really need to be planted in this way include bearded iris (not a particularly good plant for a successional scheme as it only has one season of interest, but dramatically beautiful in flower) and accent plants. A cluster of the latter can emphasise the form and colour of the flowers and seedheads, for example, the bright pink spires of *Lythrum salicaria* 'Robert' or *Veronicastrum virginicum* 'Fascination'.

In the magnolia bed to the east in the college courtyard there are large clusters of *Cimicifuga simplex* 'Brunette' standing tall against a backdrop of framing plants and contrasting with neighbouring ripples of feathery *Deschampsia cespitosa* 'Bronze Veil'. *Persicaria affinis* 'Darjeeling Red' forms a semi-evergreen mat of leaves along the edge of both sides of the path, its low, red spires lasting through the summer into the autumn. These clusters are repeated at points throughout the design. Taller blocks of *Veronicastrum virginicum* 'Temptation' and *Thalictrum rochebruneanum* benefit from the backdrop of the old wall. Dotted through the clusters are *Digitalis ferruginea*, *Verbena bonariensis* and *Aquilegia canadensis*. There are groups of bulbs for spring interest and crocuses spill out from the beds into the lawn under the spreading form of the magnolia.

The sunny bed weaves clusters into the design around the punctuating *Hebe* and the frames of *Buxus*. Species include the larger *Hydrangea* 'Annabelle' and the lower growing *Astrantia major* 'Ruby Wedding' and *Eryngium bourgatii*. Along the edge of the lawn and the narrow path, *Hylotelephium* 'Bertram Anderson'

A cluster of *Aster* x *frikartti* 'Monch' is framed by blocks of box hedging. Ripples of *Calamagrostis* x *acutiflora* 'Karl Foerster' and *Verbena bonariensis* can be seen in the background. (With special thanks to the Provost and Fellows of The Queen's College.)

A dramatic cluster *of Echinacea purpurea* 'Magnus Superior'. (With special thanks to the Provost and Fellows of The Queen's College.)

and *Persicaria affinis* 'Darjeeling Red' also create large clusters of ground cover.

Rippling

Ripples are formed of five or more plants of the same species flowing around the warp giving a dynamic, semi-natural effect whilst still allowing the designer to retain an element of control. They can cross paths or leap over the anchors, punctuation and framing plants. They can even intertwine with other ripples, changing their direction of flow. Ripples and clusters can also work together in a design; in some cases, a plant may be part of a ripple only to be a cluster in another part of the garden. This approach is most effective in a larger garden with beds big enough to accommodate sweeping swirls of planting in both the horizontal and vertical planes.

Some species work better than others when planted in ripples; they need to lend themselves to the flowing, sweeping nature of this approach. Many grasses are particularly attractive when planted in this way, as are flowers with plumes and feathery blooms that seem to

Hues of purple *Verbena bonariensis*, *Aster x frikartti* 'Monch' and *Perovskia* 'Blue Spire'. (With special thanks to the Provost and Fellows of The Queen's College.)

move in the wind. More delicate species, such as *Thalictrum delavayi*, can also be used as ripples, but it is probably better to plant them quite densely in double rows to ensure there is a flowing mass of the nodding purple flowers. Some of the less statuesque, daintier umbellifers are also great for rippling, such as *Anthriscus sylvestris* 'Ravenswing'. Species of flat-headed *Achillea* are another useful ripple: the bright yellow *Achillea* 'Cloth of Gold' is tall and robust, with long-lasting seedheads and works equally well as a ripple or a cluster.

There are several examples of ripples in the college garden. In the shady bed, the late-flowering *Anemone hupehensis* 'Hadspen Abundance' ripples in front of the *Pyracantha* frame along the wall. *A. x hybrida*

Ripples of *Perovskia* 'Blue Spire' and *Calamagrostis* x *acutiflora* 'Karl Foerster' jump across a narrow path. *Digitalis ferruginea* is dotted through the sunny bed. (With special thanks to the Provost and Fellows of The Queen's College.)

Grey-greens, silvers and purples unify this section of the garden. (With special thanks to the Provost and Fellows of The Queen's College.)

'Honorine Joubert' is also used in this bed, but in clusters – perhaps a better choice for the open flower heads. The main ripples are formed of the grass, *Deschampsia cespitosa* 'Bronze Veil'; it winds around the box and yew punctuation and crosses a cluster of the white Japanese anemones.

In the sunny bed there are many rippling plants contrasting with the low clipped box frames (clipped to heights of 90–120cm) that run through the planting as horizontal blocks in four places in the design. Ripples extend across the narrow path between the beds and occasionally even jump the box hedge. This is demonstrated by the perennial *Phlomis russeliana* and the grass *Calamagrostis* × *acutiflora* 'Karl Foerster. Other prominent ripples are formed by *Calamagrostis brachytricha*, *Perovskia* 'Blue Spire', *Scutellaria incana* and *Achillea* 'Summer Wine', the latter appearing as both a ripple and a cluster. The plan shows the colourful mass of clusters and ripples with the plants that comprise the warp left uncoloured: ripples are highlighted with coloured lines.

Interlacing

The technique of interlacing is not used in the college garden but Alex Johnson uses it in the Garden Meadow below, and I will discuss the advantages and disadvantages in more detail in later chapters. Rather than drawing up a plan, a mix of plants is specified in different proportions and they are planted randomly over a particular area of the garden. At its simplest the result is a meadow – a mosaic of random dots of colour, differing heights and leaf textures. Designers of an interlacing scheme also specify different mixes for different beds depending on the conditions. The resulting garden will have an informal, wilder atmosphere, more closely approaching the vegetation seen in nature.

The design of the warp is crucial when taking an interlacing approach: it frames the unruly mass, indicating that it is cared for and intentional; it forms a backdrop showing off the planting to best effect; it leads the eye around the garden, framing views and routes and it provides winter structure and interest.

Alex Johnson Discusses her Design for the Garden Meadow

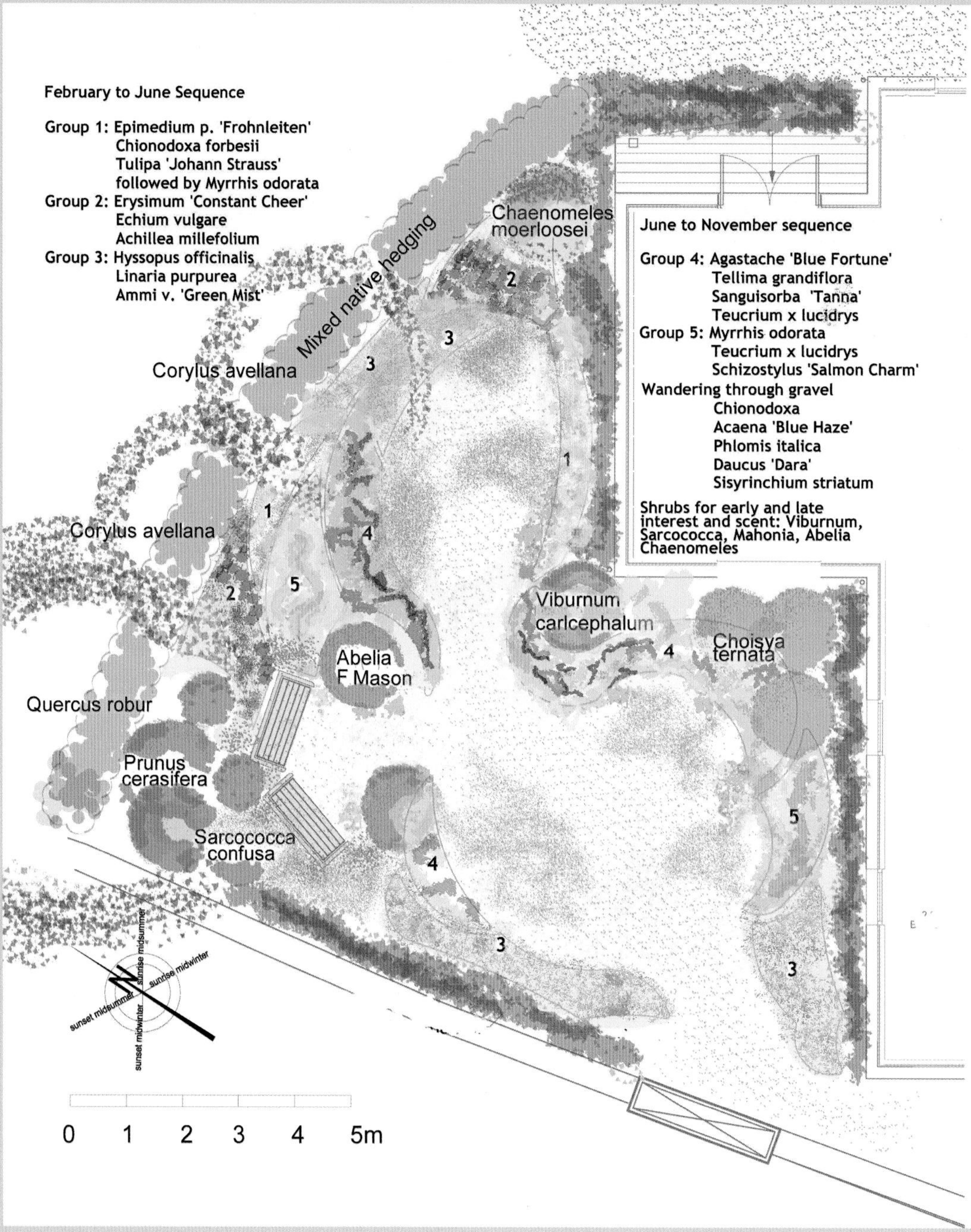

February to June Sequence

Group 1: Epimedium p. 'Frohnleiten'
Chionodoxa forbesii
Tulipa 'Johann Strauss'
followed by Myrrhis odorata
Group 2: Erysimum 'Constant Cheer'
Echium vulgare
Achillea millefolium
Group 3: Hyssopus officinalis
Linaria purpurea
Ammi v. 'Green Mist'

Corylus avellana

Mixed native hedging

Chaenomeles moerloosei

June to November sequence

Group 4: Agastache 'Blue Fortune'
Tellima grandiflora
Sanguisorba 'Tanna'
Teucrium x lucidrys
Group 5: Myrrhis odorata
Teucrium x lucidrys
Schizostylus 'Salmon Charm'
Wandering through gravel
Chionodoxa
Acaena 'Blue Haze'
Phlomis italica
Daucus 'Dara'
Sisyrinchium striatum

Shrubs for early and late interest and scent: Viburnum, Sarcococca, Mahonia, Abelia Chaenomeles

Corylus avellana

Viburnum carlcephalum

Choisya ternata

Abelia F Mason

Quercus robur

Prunus cerasifera

Sarcococca confusa

sunset midsummer
sunset midwinter
sunrise midsummer
sunrise midwinter

0   1   2   3   4   5m

Plan for the Garden Meadow designed by Alex Johnson.

The garden meadow is a scheme for a new house set in the corner of an orchard. Other parts of the garden reflect the orchard, while this section is self-contained and enclosed by a native hedge. The character of the planting is determined by interlacing groups of plants which complement each other and braid through the border and around several anchoring shrubs chosen for their early or late flowering season and for scent. The flowering sequence lasts from February, with *Epimedium*, *Viburnum* and *Chionodoxa*, as well as *Myrrhis odorata*, which emerges to cover the fading foliage of early bulbs, through to *Hesperantha* (*Schizostylis*), which lasts well into autumn.

Depending on space, the combinations could be expanded to include more umbellifers, or grasses with long-lasting seedheads – *Cenolophium* and *Pennisetum orientale*. *Festuca* 'Blue Haze' complements *Acaena* – another 'Blue Haze' which persists through the winter. Short-lived shrubby *Salvia* species would also work later in the year.

Annuals which self-seed will fill openings and plug seasonal gaps, allowing for some judicious culling and transplanting – *Nigella*, *Cerinthe* and *Briza media* are very obliging, but the latter may disperse more freely than is welcome.

Chance

Finally, there is the technique of chance and again I will discuss this in more detail in Chapter 4. All gardens are governed to a lesser or greater extent by chance, but designers might choose to let chance have a role and encourage self-seeding and the use of annuals and more ephemeral perennials among the other elements of the warp and weft. One of the problems that might occur with this method is when species self-seed into the more static plants in the warp and are then difficult to remove. Clump-forming species such as *Ruta*, *Miscanthus*, *Santolina* and *Kniphofia* are useful plants in the warp, as they do not need dividing and are less likely to let the ephemeral species seed into them (Heatherington and Sargeant, 2005).

In the college garden I use chance in a limited way, allowing some short-lived species to dot through the ripples and clusters. Examples are *Aquilegia*, three varieties of foxglove, the ever-faithful *Verbena bonariensis* and bulbs such as crocus, snowdrop and cyclamen, all of which will self-seed in certain conditions.

Seasonal Interest in the College Garden

The plan shown here gives some idea of what can be experienced in the garden in winter: the evergreen species are shown in green, and browns indicate where there are interesting seedheads. Winter flowering plants are also included. The chart that follows is more comprehensive, detailing all the plants used in the

college garden showing the seasons of interest for each. The empty boxes in spring, summer and autumn do not mean that there is nothing happening – at these times there is green foliage. In the winter column an empty box indicates that the plant is deciduous.

Winter in the college garden reveals the framing and punctuation plants. (With special thanks to the Provost and Fellows of The Queen's College.)

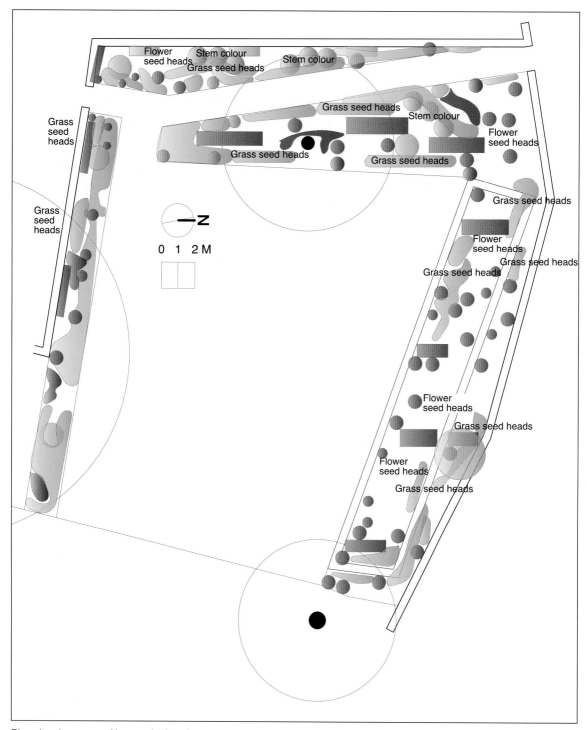

Plan showing areas of interest in the winter months.

Table 8 Seasonal interest in the college garden

	SPRING	SUMMER	AUTUMN	WINTER
TREES				
Amelanchier lamarckii	with bronze			multi-stem
Arbutus unedo		white	fruits	bark
Euonymus 'Red Cascade'			fruits	
Pyrus salicifolia 'Pendula'		silver leaf		
Sorbus hupehensis	white	grey/green	berries	
CLIMBERS AND WALL SHRUBS				
Apple (fan trained)	pink/white		fruits	form
Chaenomeles × superba 'Pink Lady'			fruits	form
Clematis 'Polish Spirit'				
Cytisus battandieri		scented	silver leaf	
Pyracantha 'Red Column'	white		berries	form
Rosa 'Ghislaine de Féligonde'		scented		
Rosa 'Gloire de Dijon'		scented		
Rosa 'Madame Alfred Carrière'		white/scented		
Rosa 'Tess of the d'Urbervilles'		scented		
Trachelospermum jasminoides		white/scented		
Wisteria sinensis	scented			
SHRUBS				
Acer palmatum 'Dissectum'				form
Berberis wilsoniae			berries	
Buxus sempervirens				form
Buxus sempervirens (box balls)				form
Choisya 'Aztec Pearl'	white			form
Cornus sanguinea 'Midwinter Fire'				
Corylus avellana 'Zellernuss'	catkins	purple leaves		coppiced
Cotinus 'Grace'				
Cotoneaster horizontalis	white		berries	
Cotoneaster suecicus 'Coral Beauty'	white		berries	
Hebe 'Autumn Glory'				
Hebe 'Mrs Winder'				
Hebe pimeleoides 'Quicksilver'		white		
Hebe rakaiensis		white		
Hebe topiaria		white		
Hydrangea 'Annabelle'		white	seedheads	
Osmanthus delavayi	white			form
Perovskia 'Blue Spire'		aromatic	silver leaf	
Pittosporum 'Irene Paterson'				
Pittosporum tenuifolium				
Pittosporum tobira	white/scented			
Pittosporum tobira 'Nanum'	white/scented			

Table 8 (*Cont'd*)

	SPRING	SUMMER	AUTUMN	WINTER
Rosa glauca			grey/green	hips
Rosmarinus officinalis	aromatic			
Sarcococca hookeriana digyna	white/scented			white
Taxus baccata				form
Taxus baccata 'Fastigiata'				form
Viburnum opulus 'Compactum'	white		berries	
PERENNIALS				
Achillea 'Summer Wine'			seedheads	
Agapanthus 'Aquamarine'			seedheads	
Agapanthus 'Midnight Star'			seedheads	
Anemone hupehensis 'Hadspen Adundance'				
Anemone × hybrida 'Honorine Joubert'			white	
Aquilegia canadensis				
Aster × frikartii 'Monch'			seedheads	
Astrantia major 'Ruby Wedding'				
Brunnera macrophylla 'Jack Frost'		silver leaf		
Cimicifuga simplex 'Brunette'		white	seedheads	
Cirsium rivulare 'Atropurpureum'			seedheads	
Digitalis ferruginea			seedheads	
Digitalis lutea			seedheads	
Digitalis purpurea 'Alba'		white seedheads		
Echinacea purpurea 'Magnus Superior'			seedheads	
Echinacea purpurea 'White Swan'		white	seedheads	
Epimedium × rubrum	bronze leaf			
Eryngium bourgatii			seedheads	
Euphorbia characias wulfenii	lime green		seedheads	
Euphorbia robbiae 'Purpurea'	lime green		seedheads	
Helleborus foetidus	lime green			lime green
Helleborus orientalis Hybrids	various			various
Heuchera americana 'Dale's Strain'				
Heuchera 'Plum Pudding'				
Liriope muscari 'Big Blue'				
Persicaria affinis 'Darjeeling Red'				
Phlomis russeliana			seedheads	
Pulmonaria 'Blue Ensign'				
Pulmonaria 'Sissinghurst White'	white	silver leaf		
Scutellaria incana				
Hylotelephium 'Bertram Anderson'				seedheads
Thalictrum rochebruneanum			seedheads	
Verbena bonariensis			seedheads	
Veronicastrum virginicum 'Temptation'			seedheads	

	SPRING	SUMMER	AUTUMN	WINTER
FERNS				
Asplenium scolopendrium Cristatum group				▨
Athyrium niponicum var. *pictum*		▨	▨	
Polystichum setiferum 'Divisilobum'				▨
Polystichum setiferum 'Herrenhausen'				▨
GRASSES				
Calamagrostis brachytricha		▨	seedheads	
Calamagrostis × *acutiflora* 'Karl Foerster'		▨	seedheads	
Deschampsia cespitosa 'Bronze Veil'		▨	seedheads	
BULBS				
Allium 'Purple Sensation'	▨	seedheads		
Camassia leichtlinii Caerulea Group	▨			
Crocus tommasinianus 'Whitewell Purple'	▨			
Crocus 'Yellow Mammoth'	▨			
Cyclamen hederifolium			▨	▨
Galanthus nivalis	white			
Narcissus 'Minnow'	▨			
Narcissus poeticus var. *recurvus*	white			
Narcissus 'Thalia'	white			
Nectaroscordum siculum	▨	seedheads		

CHAPTER 4

DIFFERENT PLANTING STRATEGIES

In the previous chapter we examined one way of designing for succession – choosing plants that have several seasons of interest and creating a planting plan using the warp and weft approach. This is a version of the mixed border that is the mainstay of many successional gardens – a combination of shrubs and herbaceous species arranged in layers.

In this chapter we will look at several techniques that can be used on their own or in combination to achieve a succession of interest and delight throughout the year.

Naturalistic Planting

In Germany in the early eighties Richard Hansen and Friedrich Stahl (1993) published their influential book, *Perennials and their Garden Habitats*, exploring the ways in which groups of perennials behaved in gardens and linking this to the ecology of species in their natural habitats. Rather than choosing plants purely for their aesthetic characteristics, they advocated selections based on ecological principles (von Schoenaich, 1994). In traditional horticulture, highly hybridised species are dependent on an intensive maintenance regime to prevent competition between each plant and its neighbours – they have to be cosseted. Wild perennials, in contrast, are better able to withstand the competitive pressures of intermingling groups of different species (Ward, 1989–90).

The New Perennial Movement in Germany drew on these principles when creating their naturalistic planting schemes. One early proponent was Rosemarie Weisse who, in 1983, designed a steppe and prairie garden at Munich Westpark on the site of a gravel pit. Visitors were able to get up close to the plants as they meandered along the winding paths through drifts of grasses and perennials (von Schoenaich, 1994). These plant communities were chosen for their ability to cope with the dry, infertile conditions and for their compatibility: they were not necessarily native species. However, many of the early naturalistic schemes relied solely on herbaceous plants and there was little in the way of structural planting or even boundaries (Lacey, 1995). Often in Germany this was not a problem as the garden was covered with snow for several months in winter (Van Groeningen, 1995), but in the milder UK climate this is an important consideration.

The term naturalistic planting is now used increasingly widely: it is often applied loosely to any scheme that has a wilder, more informal aesthetic or to designs characterised by their similarity to the groupings of plants seen in nature. In a naturalistic planting scheme, the designer can be thought of as abstracting or exaggerating nature. In reality, these schemes range across a gradient of 'naturalness'. There are those that are purely an aesthetic interpretation of the natural world; we can include many of the beautiful show gardens in this category. Then there are designers and plants people, such as Beth Chatto and Dan Pearson, who explore how plants behave in their natural habitat and apply these ideas to the choice of plants and combinations. At the opposite end of the gradient are gardens and landscapes where the designer relinquishes control completely, allowing species to self-seed without any exact idea of how the space might develop over time.

Naturalistic planting schemes can be designed to attract wildlife, as I will show in Chapter 7, but this may not always be the case. They are, however, loosely linked by their maintenance requirements; it is not true that this sort of planting design is low maintenance; rather, a different type of management is required. These schemes

This naturalistic interlacing planting scheme includes *Allium* 'Purple Sensation', *Verbascum* 'Violetta' and *Cirsium rivulare* 'Atropurpureum'. Later in the season varieties of *Geranium* and *Veronicastrum* will extend the flowering period.

emphasise plant communities rather than the individual plant, and therefore they generally require extensive maintenance methods. Instead of treating each plant as an individual, extensive maintenance treats whole groups of plants in the same way. I will return to this in Chapter 8.

Several of the techniques for seasonal succession in this chapter can be described as naturalistic; an understanding and appreciation of how plants behave in the wild underpins much of the discussion in this book, and a focus on plant groups is essential when creating any seasonal garden. One of the most important things to understand is that for a scheme to be sustainable, the competitiveness of different species must be considered (Hitchmough, 1994). Broadly speaking, plants fall into three categories: competitors, stress tolerators and ruderals (Grime, 2002). The competitors grow vigorously, especially on fertile soil, and they will respond with strong growth to the addition of nutrients. Stress tolerators, on the other hand, are slower growing, occurring in habitats where nutrients are limited. As their name suggests, they are more tolerant of adverse conditions. Finally, the opportunists, the ruderals, are short-lived, taking advantage of a change in conditions to grow vigorously and reproduce.

Soil fertility is something I will return to again, but it is worth noting that naturalistic planting schemes such as meadows require low fertility to allow the flowering species to compete with the nutrient-hungry grasses. Plants growing in less fertile soils are also less vigorous and thus there is no need for them to be staked and less likelihood that they will grow tall and swamp their smaller neighbours (*see* Chapter 6).

Anchors and accent plants, including *Cynara*, *Verbascum* and *Eremurus* bring structure to the naturalistic planting scheme at Kew Gardens, designed by Richard Wildford.

John Little's naturalistic garden uses seed mixes scattered on recycled mineral substrates.

Warp and Weft in a Gravel Garden

This garden on an infertile, dry, rocky slope in Somerset, created by Judy Pearce and Mary Payne (Heatherington and Sargeant, 2005), is an example of a design that starts with the warp and weft approach, but lets chance take a hand in determining the aesthetic into the future. The anchoring plants comprise low mounds of silvery, filigree *Artemisia alba* 'Canescens' and the purple-red leaves of *Berberis thunbergii* f. *atropurpurea* 'Atropurpurea Nana'. An earlier choice, *Artemisia ludoviciana* 'Silver Queen', was found to be too competitive and had to be removed (Heatherington and Sargeant, 2005). Clusters of perennials such as *Coreopsis verticillata, Eryngium bourgatii* and *Achillea millefolium* 'Moonshine' were added, with ripples of *Stipa tenuissima* running through the scheme. Dramatic punctuation plants – varieties of *Kniphofia* and *Verbascum* – were repeated throughout the site. It is these, together with the *Stipa*, that add the element of chance to the design as they self-seed into any gaps.

For winter interest, this garden relies on the forms of the long-lasting dead seedheads and the feathery browns of the *Stipa*, and in spring *Euphorbia myrsinites* and *Tulipa tarda* hold the attention.

Berberis thunbergii f. *atropurpurea* 'Atropurpurea Nana', *Achillea* and *Stipa tenuissima* in this garden, designed by Judy Pearce and Mary Payne.

This gravel garden, designed by Judy Pearce and Mary Payne, uses ripples, clusters and chance to create a dynamic naturalistic planting aesthetic.

Ecological Horticulture – Thomas Rainer

In their book, *Planting in a Post-Wild World*, Thomas Rainer and Claudia West (2015) explain the importance of understanding the different ecological landscapes we see around us (*see* Chapter 1) and exploring their spatial, seasonal and botanical attributes. They advocate thinking about horticulture in ecological rather than ornamental terms; designing for diversity and treating plant combinations as dynamic communities, rather than as individual species. Rainer is a US-based landscape architect and works with a simple system of layers when creating a planting scheme (Rainer, 2018): he explains how he uses two design layers – one with larger structural species and the other with plants for seasonal interest – and two functional layers of ground cover and short-lived filler species. I have discussed the idea of plant communities and layering in previous chapters and will do so again in Chapter 7 with reference to attracting wildlife into the

Table 9 Rainer's (2018) suggestions for an ecological scheme

Plant	Layer/warp and weft	Seasonal interest
Andropogon gerardii 'Red Arrow'	Structural/use as anchors or as framing plants in the warp.	A grass with tall dense tufts of leaves becoming bronze in autumn. Flowers are brownish red and become redder through the autumn.
Asclepias incarnata	Structural/use as anchors in the warp.	Clusters of lilac-purple flowers that open to white, attractive to butterflies. Flowers throughout the summer then produces narrow upright seed pods.
Sorghastrum nutans 'Indian Steel'	Structural/use as anchors in the warp.	Tall rigid stems, blue-green foliage turns yellow in autumn, bronze flowers with yellow anthers.
Amsonia ssp.	Seasonal/use in clusters in the weft.	Blue flowers are produced from late spring to midsummer. Foliage turns yellow in autumn.
Solidago rugosa 'Fireworks'	Seasonal/use in clusters in the weft.	Long-lived. Masses of yellow plumes in late summer and autumn. New foliage has a dusky red colour.
Aster ssp.	Seasonal/use in clusters or ripples in the weft.	*Aster tataricus* has pinkish-purple flowers on tall stems from September to November.
Carex ssp.	Ground cover/use as ripples or clusters in the weft or as punctuation in the warp.	There are many sedges with different coloured leaves that provide year-round interest. For variegated leaves try *Carex oshimensis* 'Evergold' or the bright green *Carex secta*.
Waldsteinia ternata	Ground cover/use as clusters in the weft.	Semi-evergreen, yellow flowers in spring and summer. Useful for shade.
Erigeron karvinskianus 'Profusion'	Filler/use as clusters in the weft and allow to dot around.	Self-seeds and flowers for months, especially if deadheaded.
Oenothera lindheimeri (*Gaura*)	Filler/use as clusters and ripples in the weft or interlace with other plants.	Flowers profusely from midsummer through autumn. Its stems and leaves are delicate so it can easily weave through other plants.

garden. The aim is to get 'the dynamics and diversity of the plant communities in balance so they can regulate themselves to an extent, thereby lowering input to keep them functioning and looking good' (Rainer, 2018: p.28). Sometimes, in order to be sustainable and reduce competitiveness, he specifies that the topsoil should be removed from the site, thus reducing fertility and encouraging a mix of shorter perennials to thrive, rather than invasive species (Rainer, 2018). I will discuss this approach further in Chapter 6.

Rainer suggests that the creative aspect of a design comes with management rather than in the earlier stages of a project and, therefore, setting expectations and understanding how plants behave in this type of scheme are both key to their success. In Table 9, I have drawn on some of Rainer's suggestions of plants suitable for these intermingling plantings and commented on how they could be used on a smaller scale in gardens, taking a warp and weft approach to the design. However, it is worth noting that in Britain the milder wet conditions early in the year can

sometimes be a problem, as not only are slugs and snails active, but also competitive cool season grasses can dominate.

Percentages – Interlacing in the Weft

In the previous chapter I introduced the technique of interlacing as a way of designing the planting of the weft. This method involves choosing a palette of plants that are then planted at random around and through the warp. The concept of interlacing most closely resembles the ways in which plants behave in nature. In Chapter 1 I suggested that we can learn from observing the vegetation of verges and under light shade in woodland when designing for succession. In order to create a similar stable scheme in the garden, we need to consider the relative heights of the species chosen, the likelihood of them flopping over, the timing of early growth in spring and the shade tolerance of the smaller plants (Hitchmough, 1994).

An interlacing combination of *Ajuga*, *Sanguisorba* and forget-me-nots. The *Sanguisorba* will grow taller as the season progresses.

In the early days of his research into the use of perennials, Nigel Dunnett explained to me how he achieved this in his own small garden (Heatherington and Sargeant, 2005). He divided the plants into five categories: structural grasses, spring, summer and autumn flowering perennials and bulbs. The early-flowering species tend to be woodland edge plants that form a carpet of green, dotted with flowers in spring, and are then content to be shaded later in the year. Examples include *Aquilegia vulgaris*, *Primula vulgaris*, *Primula veris*, *Ajuga reptans* and *Viola riviniana* Purpurea Group. These are then followed by taller-growing perennials that flower in summer and/or autumn and keep their form and seedheads into the early winter months, such as *Campanula lactiflora* and *Helianthus* 'Lemon Queen'.

In his garden, Dunnett planted a mix of species randomly, using fewer woodland edge species – 20 per cent of the mix – compared with 60 per cent of those blooming in summer and autumn. Grasses formed the remaining 20 per cent – *Calamagrostis* × *acutiflora* 'Karl Foerster', *Calamagrostis effusiflora* and *Calamagrostis* × *acutiflora* 'Eldorado' are all suitable – and bulbs were scattered over the whole area at high density (Heatherington and Sargeant, 2005).

Interlacing and Chance – Long Grass and Meadows

There are several months of the year when perennial meadows are rather uninteresting; after mowing and removing the cuttings in late autumn, the ground is a swathe of green grass and low-growing leaf rosettes until the spring. However, it is possible to design an interlacing scheme that resembles a seeded meadow while also creating a garden with year-round interest. The most obvious way is to design a warp that is attractive in the winter and to weave the meadow around the anchoring and punctuation or to frame it with clipped structural plants. Adding a high proportion of spring bulbs also extends the season of interest.

A windswept landform meadow

A more radical intervention is to design a landform meadow where mown slopes, mounds and terraces can add drama to the winter months, especially in low sunlight. The design for a windswept garden on a fairly steep slope, shown here, uses both these approaches. The site is exposed to westerly winds from the Atlantic and has been sculpted into terraces to create a gentler slope down from the house. On three sides mounds and banks have been formed to wrap the house in low swathes of wildflowers. Whips of native trees – hawthorn, blackthorn and rowan – are planted on both sides, higher up the slope, to envelop the house. These were protected from rabbits and deer, but cuttings of fuchsia and willow were pushed into the disturbed soil and left to fend for themselves. Gorse is also planted in areas on three sides of the site to add to the sense of enclosure while ensuring the views are

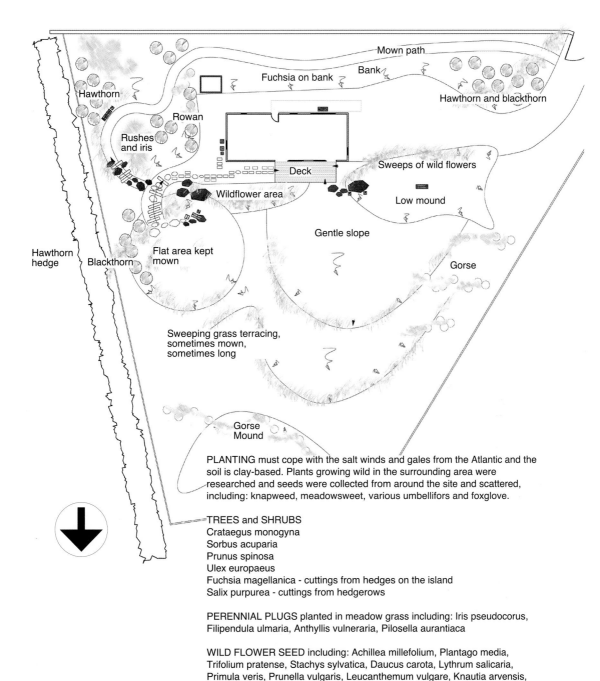

Mown path

Fuchsia on bank

Bank

Hawthorn

Hawthorn and blackthorn

Rowan

Rushes and iris

Deck

Sweeps of wild flowers

Wildflower area

Low mound

Gentle slope

Hawthorn hedge

Blackthorn

Flat area kept mown

Gorse

Sweeping grass terracing, sometimes mown, sometimes long

Gorse Mound

PLANTING must cope with the salt winds and gales from the Atlantic and the soil is clay-based. Plants growing wild in the surrounding area were researched and seeds were collected from around the site and scattered, including: knapweed, meadowsweet, various umbellifors and foxglove.

TREES and SHRUBS
Crataegus monogyna
Sorbus acuparia
Prunus spinosa
Ulex europaeus
Fuchsia magellanica - cuttings from hedges on the island
Salix purpurea - cuttings from hedgerows

PERENNIAL PLUGS planted in meadow grass including: Iris pseudocorus, Filipendula ulmaria, Anthyllis vulneraria, Pilosella aurantiaca

WILD FLOWER SEED including: Achillea millefolium, Plantago media, Trifolium pratense, Stachys sylvatica, Daucus carota, Lythrum salicaria, Primula veris, Prunella vulgaris, Leucanthemum vulgare, Knautia arvensis, Ranunculus acris, Centaurea nigra, Matricaria maritima, Rumex acetosa, Plantago lanceolata

Design by the author of a landform meadow.

Low light in winter catches the mounds and terraces of the mown meadow.

Grasses glow in the evening light.

not obstructed. A native wildflower seed mix was scattered randomly in parts of the garden and a few plant plugs were added to this seed mix, the most successful being meadowsweet and yellow flag.

On the whole, this garden has been left to its own devices, allowing a high element of chance into the design. Over the years there have been issues with docks and thistles and yet the trees, shrubs and wildflowers continue to thrive. As it approaches its third decade, bracken and nettles are becoming more of a problem and it may be that a more radical intervention becomes necessary in order to maintain the diversity of the flora and fauna found here.

Ox-eye daisies self-seed around the landscape. Paths are mown through the grassy meadow.

A ridge and furrow meadow

The second example of interlacing and chance takes a more prescribed approach than the example above. The site in Suffolk, owned by the Royal Society for the Protection of Birds (RSPB) was designed together with my colleague Alex Johnson. The garden slopes down from a visitor centre to the wooded banks of the River Stour; the conditions varied across this area, allowing us to use a range of different wildflower seed mixes to create a diverse meadow. To give interest in the winter months we created mounds running down the slope, reminiscent of a ridge and furrow system seen in the surrounding landscape; this also allowed us to vary the substrate composition and thus the seed mix. The larger grassy flowering areas were created with a mix of 75:25 topsoil and river-washed sand to a depth of 150mm. In all, the resulting garden has six different types of habitats across the seeded meadow:

- Rough grass and flowering lawn, including slow-growing grasses such as highland bent, slender-creeping red fescue and smooth-stalked meadow grass, together with wildflowers that respond well to some mowing – examples include lady's bedstraw, ox-eye daisy, cowslip, meadow buttercup and red clover.
- Mown grass and flowering lawn seeded with the same mix as above but mown more frequently.
- Double meadow ridge built up with 10mm flint gravel mixed with 25 per cent loam-based topsoil and seeded with deep-rooted species that prefer infertile, sandy, well-drained soils. Examples include yarrow, viper's bugloss, bird's foot trefoil, ribwort plantain and bladder campion. The ridge was also seeded with a cornfield mix of annuals to give interest in the first year before the perennials established.

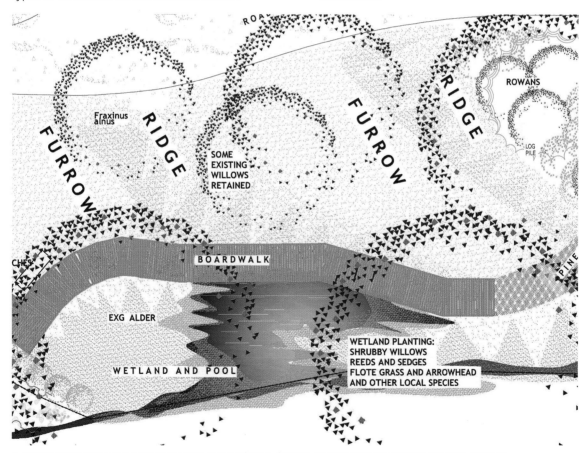

A sketch of the ridge and furrow meadow at the RSPB in Suffolk, designed by the author with Alex Johnson.

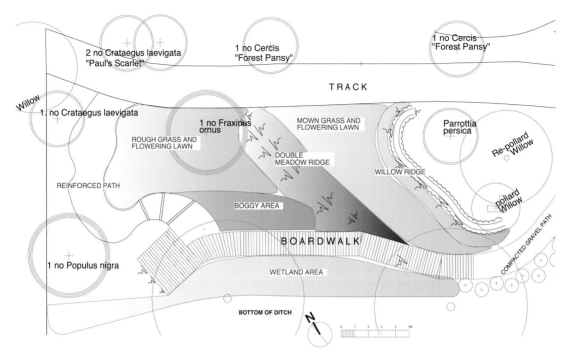

Plan of the RSPB meadow designed by the author with Alex Johnson showing the position of the different seed mixes.

The ridge and furrow meadow and boardwalk at the RSPB garden.

Diversity of species in the meadow ridge at the RSPB garden.

- Willow ridge constructed of living willow spiling, built up with 10mm flint gravel mixed with 50 per cent topsoil and seeded with a flowering lawn mix of perennials with no additional grasses.
- Boggy area where there is a natural spring, seeded with the flowering lawn species above and a mix suitable for the margins of ponds and ditches including knapweed, meadowsweet and red campion.
- Wetland area at the bottom of the slope seeded with a mix of the pond edge species in the boggy area and a wet meadow mix that will cope with periods of flooding and dry conditions in summer, including wild carrot, hedge bedstraw, common sorrel and ragged robin.

These varied habitats attract a diverse range of wildlife and also provide interest through the seasons. In winter the willow spiling and mature trees frame the meadow and the ridge and furrow design catches the light and directs the view down through the trees to the flooded river below.

Creating Matrices

I mentioned Piet Oudolf when discussing designing with clusters in Chapter 3. He is well known for the way in which he combines large blocks of individual herbaceous plants and then repeats these combinations around the site. This method works best in large gardens and public spaces where many varieties can be combined in ways to give the maximum colour and texture through the summer and autumn.

Oudolf also uses a technique he calls matrix planting. This design approach is a type of naturalistic planting that more closely resembles a meadow. He selects lower growing species in muted colours and with less distinctive forms for the matrix; these create a dense and homogeneous cover across the expanse of the garden. The choice of plant is determined by its competitiveness – it should not out-compete the primary plants that will grow up and through the matrix – and its resilience and persistence: the mass of matrix plants must have structure and interest over a major part of the year (Greenbee landscapes, 2019). Grasses are a staple of the matrix (Hoffman, 2013):

feathery *Stipa tenuissima* that catches the slightest breeze; wispy plumes of *Deschampsia cespitosa* 'Goldtau'; cultivars of *Panicum virgatum* that have red highlights, *Molinia caerulea* varieties and *Sporobolus heterolepis* with its sprays of airy flowers, yellow and orange autumn tones and long-lasting leaves and seedheads. In several schemes the latter is used on its own to form the matrix. It is durable, long-lived and adds a diffuse, hazy appearance to the overall planting.

Layered into the matrix Oudolf specifies repeating primary plants that rise above the sea of grass, emerging as dramatic features that keep their structure into the autumn. Although he claims that colour is not as important as form and texture, the species he chooses all give seasonal drama when in flower with their wonderful contrasting shades and tones.

At the Hauser and Wirth garden in Somerset (Gardens Illustrated, n.d.) (Dusoir, 2019) key primary plants include *Doellingeria umbellata*, its daisy-like white flowers held 1.5m high on stiff stems, the rose-pink bottlebrush flowers of *Sanguisorba* 'Blackthorn' and the red dots of *S. officinalis* 'Red Buttons', both of which flower from summer through to early autumn. There is also *Echinacea pallida* with long, pale pink, reflexed petals that droop from the central burnt-orange cone. As the petals lose their colour, they become more ethereal until the brown button of the cone is all that remains. In autumn dramatic colours (House and Garden, n.d.) include the blood-red stems and orange leaves of *Aruncus* 'Horatio', the upright

pale brownish-orange *Molinia caerulea* 'Moorhexe' and also the luminous feathery acid-yellow leaves of *Amsonia hubrichtii* or the more lemony yellow of *A. tabernaemontana* var. *salicifolia*.

Finally, there are the scatter plants: these are placed randomly as the name implies, breaking up the loose rhythm of the primary planting, and are often ephemeral species, self-seeders and bulbs.

To create a successful scheme using this technique of matrix planting, a designer needs to understand the relative competitiveness of plants and how this relates to the conditions on site. It is a difficult approach to take in smaller gardens as it requires plenty of space to include both the mass of grassy matrix and a large selection of emergent species. There is also little or no winter interest once the seedheads have succumbed to the rains and before the bulbs appear. In my experience, grasses such as *Deschampsia* and *Panicum* lose their seedheads fairly early in the winter. With the warmer, wetter winters that are predicted over the coming decades in the UK, the dramatic effects of skeleton seedheads glistening with frost in the low winter sun may be a rare sight and it may be advisable to modify the principles of the matrix and include some trees and shrubby planting. However, the matrix approach can result in a beautiful garden for three seasons of the year, packed with interest, dynamism and atmosphere. Those of us working with smaller gardens can experiment with some of the combinations and juxtapositions Oudolf creates, and observe the species that cope best with the winter conditions.

A Forest Garden

A forest garden is one in which layers of edible and other functional species (for dyes or medicinal purposes) are planted and managed in a sustainable way that mimics the ecosystems of woodland edges. It is a system that is based on layering plants from the tree or canopy layer, down through the shrub layers to perennials and ground cover. I will discuss layers further with reference to attracting wildlife in Chapter 7. Although primarily designed as a way of growing food crops sustainably, I see no reason why we should not learn from this method of gardening when planting for more aesthetic purposes,

or ideally, mixing the two. According to proponents of forest gardening, many ornamental perennials are edible, hostas and daylilies are given as examples (Agroforestry Research Trust, n.d.); but be careful when experimenting and always take expert advice. There is also the benefit to the environment; in designing with layers that cover the ground and become self-sustaining, we are storing carbon in the soil and removing it from the air, so helping to mitigate the climate crisis.

The Triangle Community Garden, www.trianglegarden.org, planted a forest garden over ten years ago and Vicky Wyer, a trustee, discussed with me how this space has evolved. Many of the plants I mention here have been successful in the garden, which is just north of London, and always open to the public, so has to be very resilient. Martin Crawford (Agroforestry Research Trust, n.d.), a proponent of this system of gardening, explains that:

'Diversity is extremely important because it creates resilience. That means diversity of structure as well as diversity of species. A perennial-based diverse system should have few pest or disease problems and also be fairly unaffected by climate extremes' (Crawford, 2014: p.27).

In a small garden start with a top fruiting tree, *see* the section on orchards and fruit trees in Chapter 7, or choose a nut tree such as almond or cobnut. American elder, *Sambucus canadensis*, is another possible choice, flowering throughout the summer. It can be used to make elderflower cordial, but unlike our native elder, it does not have any berries. At the community garden they also grow the Sichuan Pepper, *Zanthoxylum schinifolium*, which can be used as a shrub, small tree, or a multi-stem, with compound leaves and creamy flowers in spring (Glanville, 2019). The red fruits ripen in autumn and split open to reveal the seeds inside and the leaves turn vivid yellow in the autumn. It is the spicy seed cases that are harvested and used in Asian cuisine. The leaves, bark and fruit all have a distinctive aromatic spicy, citrusy scent.

In a larger garden there will be space for more than one tree, but the aim is to ensure that there are gaps in the canopy where light can enter, even when the tree matures. If the shade becomes too dense, the understorey plants will not thrive: in this case, the crown of the tree can be raised in order to let more light in. Many soft fruit bushes cope with semi-shade so there is a wide choice of gooseberries, raspberries, tayberries, loganberries, blackcurrants or more unusual varieties such as Siberian honeyberry, and the ornamental Japanese wineberry which has tiny, tasty, jewel-like fruit and rusty furred stems. For the seasonal successional garden, *Fuchsia magellanica* with its pretty, scarlet flowers throughout the summer and its edible fruits is a great choice. The ground cover layer is where more ornamental species can be included, such as fennel, globe artichoke, alpine strawberries and, if it is damp enough, Ostrich fern, which apparently has edible young fronds if they are cooked (make sure you take advice before sampling unusual species). Herbs and plants that provide dyes, such as the annual dyer's coreopsis, and dyer's chamomile can also be planted in this layer (Crawford, 2014). Beth Chatto recommends a variety of the latter that flowers all summer, *Anthemis tinctoria* 'E.C. Buxton', which has ferny green leaves and pretty pale yellow daisy-like flowers.

Finally, it is important to include species that increase soil fertility such as nitrogen fixers – species of *Alnus* and *Elaeagnus* – and those with deep roots that raise minerals found in the subsoil up into the topsoil layer – comfreys and sorrels (Agroforestry Research Trust, n.d.).

Japanese wineberry and daylilies.

Starting from Winter

The grey, wet winters that characterise the UK climate often mean that much of the garden becomes a soggy mass of brown: dead and dying plants start to rot in mounds, surrounded by fallen leaves, and deciduous shrubs in dull light do not do much to relieve the gloominess of the scene. However, it is important to understand that dormancy and death are natural stages in the yearly cycle and dying vegetation has a part to play in the habitats of the garden, as I will discuss in Chapter 7.

One approach to planning a successional garden is to start from winter. When designing the warp we can pay particular attention to the winter form, colour and detail of each of the anchoring and punctuation plants and site these in positions that draw attention away from the mass of dead perennials, the empty vegetable beds or the bare boundary fences. It is also important to consider the views out from the house as often this is the only part of the garden that is on show for the winter months. Small-leafed evergreen shrubs are

Eranthis hyemalis with snowdrops in semi-shade under trees.

particularly useful for creating sculptural frames that catch the eye, becoming a seasonal focal point for a few months of the year before doubling as a backdrop to the summer grasses and perennials.

Planting evergreens is an easy way to provide this winter interest, but not all evergreens are equal; grey-leafed plants, such as lavender and cistus, sometimes look dismal in the damp, grey light of January and February. In late autumn *Helleborus orientalis* leaves begin to discolour and lie prostrate along the ground and *Bergenias* do not seem to like clay soils and the leaves in winter are often chewed and unsightly. Although the latter are said to do well in shade, I have seen them looking healthy in Beth Chatto's garden on free-draining soil and in an open situation. Some, such as *Bergenia* 'Arbendglut' and *B. crassifolia* 'Autumn Red', have bright red and maroon autumn colouring. Chatto (1978) also advocates using *Helleborus lividus* subsp. *corsicus*, otherwise known as *Helleborus argutifolius*, for round-the-year interest. It starts producing apple-green flowers in winter and continues through to May, as well as forming large clumps of evergreen leaves with a hint of cool blue-grey colouring, and it is a good choice for a low-growing anchor in the warp.

Once a selection of anchoring, punctuation and framing plants is drawn up in draft, we can begin to build up the planting design in layers that come forward from the back of the bed. Rather than planting small bulbs near the front, those which are light in colour can be sited further back, perhaps at the base of a tree or a hedge; their dying leaves will be hidden by the new growth of the herbaceous species later in the spring. It is worth remembering that small, darker coloured flowers get lost if they are too far away, so these should be nearer the front of the bed. Then begin to layer the other plants in the weft, starting with those that are lower growing and early flowering that will then be shaded by the taller, later-flowered species. In this way, there may even be taller perennials towards the front of a bed rather than at the back. Some of the semi-transparent species discussed in Chapter 2 would work well in this sort of scheme.

Table 10 Bulbs and corms for a seasonal succession scheme

Bulb/corm	Comments	In combination
Early spring interest		
Crocus tommasinianus C. aureus	Early flowering purple and yellow crocus both grow well in lawns and should happily seed themselves around.	This colourful display can brighten the space under deciduous shrubs.
Eranthis hyemalis	Winter aconites are the first flowers to emerge in spring and form a carpet under trees and shrubs.	Plant in large groups under deciduous trees where they can catch the early spring sunlight.
Fritillaria meleagris	The snake's head fritillary has unusually marked maroon-purple bell-shaped flowers.	It looks wonderful naturalised in long grass, where summer-flowering annuals and perennials also thrive to extend the season of interest.
Galanthus nivalis	Snowdrops are happy to be shaded later in the year and therefore can be planted under deciduous shrubs and trees, as well as among large-leafed perennials and ferns. If left to their own devices, snowdrops will seed into gaps amongst established plants where it would be almost impossible to plant anything.	Try planting a mat of snowdrops with Ajuga reptans 'Catlin's Giant' under a multi-stemmed Cercis canadensis 'Forest Pansy'.
Later spring interest		
Allium christophii	Dramatic starbursts of pinkish purple. Leaves die before flowering.	When planted among the emerging, grey-green shoots of taller Hylotelephium ssp. the dying leaves are hidden by the early new growth.
Allium 'Purple Sensation' or A. 'Purple Rain'	The dying leaves are not attractive so they can be hidden among the similarly textured leaves of Hemerocallis.	Look lovely planted among a mass of forget-me-nots. The purple flowers and then the dead seedheads of larger alliums look good in combination with silver-leafed Stachys ssp.
Allium schoenoprasum var. sibiricum	A large chive that can be planted in the herb bed or in combination with perennials.	Combines well with low grey-green leaves and long-lasting magenta flowers of Geranium 'Russell Pritchard' (Lloyd, 2021).
Gladiolus communis subsp. byzantinus	Native of the Mediterranean so needs light soil and full sun.	Dramatic vertical accents of magenta-pink spires that combine well with silver and grey-leafed plants.
Autumn interest		
Crocus speciosus autumn crocus	Useful in autumn in rough grass and amongst shrubs or in front of a hedge.	Plant at the base of multi-stem trees to add interest.
Colchicum autumnale	Prefers a sunny position. Flowers appear on naked stems in autumn. By spring the leaves can grow quite large and may overpower smaller growing spring bulbs.	Can be grown in pots or in gravel beds. Will grow under deciduous trees and shrubs as long as they get some sun.
Cyclamen hederifolium Silver Leafed Group	Leaves appear in winter and spring then die back. Flowers in autumn.	Useful at the base of hedges and under shrubs. If planted with Cyclamen orbiculatum you will have two seasons of flowers.
Leucojum autumnale	The autumn snowflake likes moist soil and an open sunny site. Delicate white flowers over a long period.	Best in a scree or rock garden where the bell-like flowers can be seen to good effect.
Nerine ssp.	Dormant in summer before flowering on erect, leafless stems in autumn. The leaves appear after flowering. Water if there is no rain to encourage flowering.	Bright autumn colours, so best against a backdrop of green foliage, grasses or in pots.

Colchicum autumnale under multi-stemmed *Euonymus sachalinensis* in the garden at Sissinghurst.

Pots and Planters

Planters and containers can be used to add another layer of interest to the successional garden; it is even possible to move a pot to fill an unforeseen gap in a bed for a few weeks. If you only have a small space, you can achieve a more dramatic effect by having one large pot or planter, rather than lots of little ones. In this case, planting a tree with a sculptural form and autumn colour, such as one of the many Japanese maples, is a great choice. It can be underplanted with low-growing bulbs or ferns and will provide year-round interest.

Alternatively, to have a range of flowering plants in pots and planters through the seasons, several pots can be rotated: in winter, clipped evergreens and ferns provide form and structure; spring bulbs, especially tulips, can be planted with later flowering annuals; *Agapanthus* and *Allium* 'Purple Sensation' planted together provide colour for early to mid- summer; grasses such as *Imperata cylindrica rubra, Festuca glauca* and *Poa labillardierei* look good combined with *Knautia macedonica, Scabiosa caucasia* 'Perfecta Blue' or *Dianthus carthusianorum*; *Salvia* 'Amistad' provides summer colour that lasts into autumn and contrasts with the dying flower heads of *Calamagrostis brachytricha*.

Often pots are planted up for colour in the summer months and the choice of annuals is extensive, so I will just give a few suggestions here. Start with a framework of textural leaves, the silver-leafed *Helichrysum petiolare* perhaps, and add pale

blue-mauve *Convolvulus mauritanicus* to trail over the edges of the pot – it blooms from June through to the end of September. Nasturtiums are a mainstay of container planting and come in a mass of bright, hot colours to contrast with blue *Lobelia erinus* and there is also a climbing variety, *Tropaeolum tuberosum* 'Ken Aslet' to give height. If you can provide a support for climbers against a wall at the back of the container the dramatic deep-pink tender perennial Glory lily, *Gloriosa* 'Rothschildiana' flowers all summer. Another climber, the scented *Trachelospermum jasminoides*, will be happy in pots for years and keeps its glossy leaves in winter. This can then be combined with annuals and bulbs to add colour.

Sarah Raven's website, www.sarahraven.com, has plenty of ideas – both annuals and perennials – for pots and planters: after the last frosts, she suggests planting a mix of trailing *Verbena* × *superbena* 'Burgundy' with *V. canadensis* 'Homestead Purple' and *V. rigida* that in full sun will last well into November. Many of the annuals I mention below are also suitable and some continue flowering for long periods if they are deadheaded.

These dramatic Corten pots in a small front garden are surrounded by box and lavender and filled with *Festuca glauca*.

Salvia 'Amistad' contrasting with the dying flower heads of *Calamagrostis brachytricha* in early autumn.

Growing from Seed

Using annuals to provide seasonal variation is relatively cheap, although when raising plants from seed there is a high rate of attrition. Many annuals have a long flowering season and give a burst of colour and freshness to the garden when shrubs may just be settling into their mid-green summer foliage and bulbs have finished blooming. They are also useful for filling gaps around shrubs in a newly planted garden.

There are early summer-flowering annuals and biennials such as aquilegias, foxgloves, love-in-a-mist, opium poppies and honesty, all of which develop seedheads that provide interest later in the season. An especially unusual honesty is *Lunaria annua* var. *albiflora* 'Alba Variegata' with its white flowers and variegated leaves as well as the characteristic silver seedheads. How these annuals are used will depend on the style of the garden. Hardy annuals can be left to self-seed amongst the shrubs and perennials, but there will always be an element of chance to this approach; seeds may not germinate or may be too successful with the result that they dominate the garden (this is often the case with the brightly coloured yellow and orange Welsh poppy). It may be desirable to collect the seed and sow it in a patch where you would like the plants to grow next year. Or, in order to have even more control, seed can be germinated in pots and then planted out in a designated space. Some annuals can be planted in autumn to give them a head start the following year (Heatherington and Johnson, 2022). If you plan to grow annuals in a designated section of the garden, you can try using a no-dig approach (Mogendorff and Romain, 2022) (*see* Chapter 6).

Lloyd (2021) suggests using two annuals to provide a display of low-growing successional flowering. One of his mini combinations includes the upright *Omphalodes linifolia*, which has a grey-green leaf and white flowers that bloom in late spring and early summer. He combines this with *Convolvulus tricolor* – its blue flowers succeeding the white. It also helps to support the straggling stems of the *Omphalodes* later in the season. Or you could try planting *Phacelia tanacetifolia*, loved by bees and used as a green manure, with Californian poppies that will flower for several months. Adding *Echium vulgare* 'Blue Bedder' to the mix gives a truly pollinator-friendly combination.

Lower-growing plants such as marigolds, flower for long periods if deadheaded and come in a range of brilliant colours. There are the mahogany-crimson *Tagetes patula* 'Linnaeus Burning Embers' and *Tagetes tenuifolia* 'Red Gem' – both excellent companion plants for growing around tomatoes – and the orange English marigold, *Calendula officinalis* 'Indian Prince'. The Chinese forget-me-not, *Cynoglossum amabile* 'Firmament' provides a mass of delicate azure-blue flowers that are good for cutting and contrast well with whites and oranges in the front of a border. If allowed to go to seed, the dried seedheads are also interesting. Another blue is *Isotoma axillaris* 'Blue Star', an invaluable bushy plant for containers with toothed leaves and star-like flowers from late spring to autumn.

Taller annuals often used in pots are the many varieties of *Cosmos bipinnatus* that flower from July through to October. Gaps at the back of a bed can also be filled with the deep velvety-purple *Salvia* 'Amistad' that will flower into November. Purple salvias contrast beautifully with the night-scented, acid-green *Nicotiana alata* 'Lime Green'. Snapdragons such as *Antirrhinum majus* 'Appleblossom' and 'White Giant' are statuesque accent plants that are also good cut flowers and will keep producing blooms into October, as long as they are cut to a pair of leaves rather than to the ground.

Flowers with an open daisy-like form include *Tithonia rotundiflora* 'Torch', the Mexican sunflower, that has

A bee circles round and round drinking nectar from a sunflower – *Helianthus* Pro-cut 'White Nite'.

large scarlet and orange flowers from midsummer through autumn, carried on tall stems up to 1.5m in height. Another brightly coloured tall daisy is *Venidium fastuosum* 'Jaffa Ice', otherwise known as the monarch of the veldt. Its black-centred orange and white flower heads add drama throughout the summer. There are also many different and subtle-coloured varieties of sunflower: *Helianthus debilis* 'Vanilla Ice' has the palest yellowy-cream flowers and *H. annuus* 'Pro-cut Plum' is a soft dusky crimson with a hint of cappuccino.

Finally, there are the delicate white umbellifers, especially *Orlaya grandiflora*, which contrasts beautifully with *Allium* 'Purple Sensation' in early summer, and later you can plant *Ammi majus* and *A.*

visnaga 'Compact White' with their feathery, frothy leaves to continue the theme.

Annuals can be included in the design of the weft in the form of ripples and clusters, but they can also be placed to appear as if they have seeded by chance. Plant several of one species close together and then dot smaller groups around the main cluster and individuals even further away. The effect is of a plant that has dispersed naturally from the parent colony. This is also a good way of planting bulbs. It is important to remember that annuals usually have little winter presence, but they do provide a long flowering season and allow the designer and gardener to be creative, making changes from year to year.

A southern hawker dragonfly rests on a twig among the *Orlaya grandiflora* and *Briza media.*

CHAPTER 5

CHOOSING PLANTS FOR THE SEASONS

This chapter focuses on the seasons – winter, spring, summer and autumn – and for each, examines the characteristics of plants that lend themselves to a seasonal succession design approach. In the UK we are lucky to have conditions that enable us to design gardens that mark the changes in season and celebrate the differences that these bring. From the dormancy of winter with its low light and stark forms, the new growth of spring gradually emerges, then there are the speedy changes in colours, textures and masses that occur in May and June, before a gradual slowing through the hotter summer months. Canopies close overhead and the shade becomes denser rather than dappled. Finally, autumn blazes into colour and light levels change again, often creating dramatic backlit effects and short-lived contrasts of colour and texture.

We can design our gardens to take advantage of these changes, marking the seasons explicitly while also ensuring there are long periods of beauty, activity and development that delight the people who use the garden and provide shelter and food for wildlife, as I will discuss in Chapter 6.

Winter

As suggested in the previous chapter, it can be helpful to start a design with the winter in mind and I also discussed some of the bulbs we can use to bring interest to a garden in the early months of the year. Chapter 2 includes a section on scented winter flowers and below I look at some of the other attributes of plants that provide excitement in the colder, dormant period.

Ice on winter flowering honeysuckle.

Form – Trees and Shrubs

Trees with their sculptural forms make good focal points; some even carry the traces of the prevailing weather in their branches as they bend away from the wind. There are several ways in which we can enhance these shapes through pruning and traditional techniques such as coppicing and pollarding. They can be trained as multi-stemmed forms and we can raise the crown on the more commonly shrubby species or even create formal topiary and try cloud-training and pleaching (*see* Chapter 8).

Some shrubs have interesting forms in winter without requiring any pruning. *Acer palmatum* 'Dissectum' is beautiful throughout the year with its feathery leaves and autumn colour, but in winter the bent, gnarled and swirling branches have their own attraction, especially when underplanted with bulbs such as snowdrops or crocus. *Pinus mugo* is another low-growing shrub with an architectural form and can be used in combination with the Japanese maple. It is recommended that in order to keep the pine in shape you should not use shears or secateurs, but instead should take the time-consuming approach of picking out each growing tip individually (Architectural Plants, 2023b).

Hedges also provide winter interest; in summer they serve as a backdrop or frame to colourful perennials and grasses, but in the winter the hedge is a structure commanding attention through its overall form as well as drawing the eye to the detailed texture of evergreen or dead and dying leaves. It is worth remembering that beech and hornbeam hedges keep their dead leaves over winter. When there is little else to look at, clipped hedges are important sculptural elements in a design whilst a more shaggy, natural-looking hedge is a valuable wildlife habitat.

Evergreen forms and the stark shapes of trunk and branches are enhanced by the low winter light at West Dene Gardens.

Variegated and Colourful Evergreens

Shrubs with variegated evergreen leaves can be placed to bring colour to shady parts of the garden and to lighten up dull days. These need to be chosen with care and used in moderation; those with extreme levels of variegation and colour do not have a place in more informal or naturalistic schemes. However, a low-growing shrub such as *Euonymus* × *fortunei* 'Emerald Gaiety' with its silver and green foliage is a useful ground cover in shade and contrasts later in the year with the pale purple flowers of *Vinca minor* or the lime green of *Alchemilla mollis*. For a sunny patch, there are several subtly variegated thymes, the creamy-yellow margined *Thymus* 'Hartington Silver' and the golden *T.* 'Golden Lemon' are good examples, although in wet soils they do not last through the winter.

The yellow-leafed *Choisya ternata* 'Sundance' is not a plant I would choose to place in the sun where its bright colour seems particularly artificial, or can be bleached out to a strange pale yellow, but sited in semi-shade the leaves take on a more subtle limey-green tone that combines well with darker evergreens. Another shrub with lime-green leaves for shade, is the low, dome-shaped *Skimmia* × *confusa* 'Kew Green' with its beautifully scented flowers in spring. The flowers of *Helleborus foetidus* look especially good with this *Skimmia*.

I mentioned *Pittosporum* and *Daphne* in a previous chapter: variegated examples of these that bring light to the winter garden are *Pittosporum tenuifolium* 'Variegatum' and *Daphne odora* 'Aureomarginata'. *Elaeagnus* × *ebbingei* 'Limelight' is easy to grow in more difficult situations and *Ilex* 'Golden King' is a striking holly of the female variety, therefore producing red berries as well.

As well as gold and silver variegations, there are shrubs with pink- and purple-tinged leaves that might suit certain designs but be careful where you site these: shrubs with deep purple leaves, such as *Pittosporum* 'Tom Thumb' absorb rather than reflect the light, leaving a dark hole in the scene on a gloomy day instead of enlivening the view. There are also the grey and silver-leafed plants that have lilac and purple flowers in summer, such as *Lavandula angustifolia* 'Hidcote', *Lavandula stoechas* and *Teucrium fruticans*. These contrast well with purple leaves or with the dead flower stems of grasses and are also a good choice for pots or a balcony.

Finally, there are a few evergreen perennials and grasses with different coloured leaves that can add interest through the winter months. *Libertia peregrinans* consists of striking fans of narrow, stiff leaves that appear bright orange and look lovely in a gravel bed, especially when combined with low growing bulbs such as scillas or the smaller alliums. *Euphorbia pithyusa* is not totally hardy but will self-seed and forms mounds of blue leaves with the bonus of green flowers in summer. The prostrate mounds of *Euphorbia myrsinitis* have silver-blue leaves and lime-green flowers in spring and there is also the blue grass, *Festuca glauca* 'Elijah Blue' with leaves that need little attention accept a comb now and again. For a golden colouration try the sedges, *Carex oshimensis* 'Evergold' or *Carex elata* 'Aurea'.

A winter view of the garden shown at the beginning of this chapter. The yew hedge forms a backdrop to the unusual wisteria seed pods and the dead grasses.

Winter details (clockwise from top left): *Polystichum* and *Epimedium*, male yew flowers, *Parrotia persica* flowers, *Euphorbia characias* subsp. *wulfenii*, willow stems, and dead flower heads of *Hydrangea* 'Annabelle'.

Stems and Bark

The bark and stems of trees and shrubs can provide welcome colour and texture to the winter garden. Some shrubs have yellow, orange, red, purple, white and even nearly black stems. Judicious pruning and traditional techniques of coppicing and pollarding can ensure that these stems are displayed to their best advantage. As well as drawing attention with their attractive winter shapes, the tactile nature of tree trunks is a joy throughout the year and can also provide visual interest, even when viewed from the house. The bark may range from bright white, through pale greens and orangey browns to chestnut reds.

The striking bark of *Prunus serrula* (above right), *Acer griseum* (left) and a snake-bark maple (right).

The table below gives just a few of the best examples of trees with wonderful bark and shrubs with colourful stems.

Table 11 Trees and shrubs for winter interest

Tree/shrub	Attributes for the seasonal garden
Interesting bark	
Acer griseum	Chestnut-red paper bark and a domed shape. Red and orange autumn colour.
Acer rufinerve 'Erythrocladum'	A cultivar of the snake-bark maple with pink buds and unusual golden-yellow new growth. The leaves turn red and yellow in autumn.
Acer striatum	A snake-bark maple with green and white striped marking. Yellow autumn colour.
Arbutus × *andrachnoides*	A cross between two species of *Arbutus*. Requires good drainage. Evergreen with masses of white flowers and flaky red bark. Does not often have fruit. Try *Arbutus unedo* if you would like to have the strawberry-like fruits as well.
Betula nigra	Peeling pale brown trunk, long catkins in spring and good autumn colour.
Betula utilis subsp. *jacquemontii* 'Grayswood Ghost'	A birch with bright white bark, catkins in spring and a little autumn colour.
Eucalyptus pauciflora subsp. *debeuzevillei*	Grow as a multi-stem – the stems never grow as straight trunks (Architectural Plants, 2023a). Known as the snow gum with white stems and glaucous blue leaves. Does not like competition but, if happy, will grow very fast.
Prunus serrula	Glossy, shining mahogany bark with some slight peeling as it grows. The most tactile of the trees in this list.
Winter stem colour	
Cornus alba 'Elegantissima'	A dogwood with creamy variegated leaves that bring light to shady places. The stems are a dark red.
Cornus alba 'Siberica'	Bright crimson stems, creamy-white flowers in summer and reddish leaves in autumn. Good for pollinators.

Tree/shrub	Attributes for the seasonal garden
Cornus sanguinea 'Anny's Winter Orange'	Red-tipped, orange-red stems, orange-yellow autumn colour. A slightly smaller species of dogwood, but should still be cut back in spring to encourage the amazingly colourful stems.
Rubus cockburnianus	The new growth is burnished with red and it forms a mass of shining white stems. Cut back to ground level in early spring.
Salix alba var. *vitellina* 'Britzensis'	A willow with orangey-coral stems. Can be cut back each year and is fast growing, making 2m (6½ft) of growth in a season.

Betula utilis subsp. *jacquemontii* with an underplanting of ferns and foxgloves at Markshall Estate in Essex.

Pruning for colourful stems

Traditionally coppicing was used to create a supply of timber and firewood; the long straight new growth that sprang up from the base of the plant was suitable for constructing fences and other structures. Hazel and sweet chestnut were commonly coppiced, but it is a useful technique for many species. Nowadays there is less call for the supply of coppiced wood, but the practice is carried out to let light into the understorey in woodland and to increase wildlife diversity through the creation of varied habitats (National Trust, n.d.).

Although coppicing usually takes place in February and early March, in order to keep the colourful stems for winter interest for as long as possible, pruning can be delayed until late March and April. Young shrubs need a couple of years to establish their root system before you undertake any hard pruning. When coppicing shrubs such as dogwoods, the stems are cut down to within 10cm of the ground and side shoots can also be pinched out to encourage new bushy growth. Pollarding is a slightly different technique and is more often used for willows; in this case a trunk is allowed to form, and the stems cut to about 60–90cm from ground level. For more vigorous species of dogwood and willow, coppicing and pollarding can take place each year, but for others every two or three years is sufficient. Sometimes it is suggested that one third of the stems are cut back on a rotation basis rather than cutting back the whole plant.

Light Levels

In Chapter 1 we looked at how light levels under trees determine what grows in the ground layer and I have also touched on how low sunlight can bring atmosphere to the dormant winter garden.

As designers and gardeners, we need to be aware of the shade cast by hedges, fences and walls and the ways in which these barriers not only restrict light levels, but also create rain shadows where the soil is especially dry. Often plants growing in these situations stretch towards the light and thus, in turn, shade lower-growing plants nearer the front of the border. Staking taller plants can help to mitigate this, but it also makes sense to select species that cope better with dry shade. These may be lower-growing species that come into their own in the successional garden in winter and spring, as the taller species in front of them lose their leaves or die back. In fact, for leaf growth to be healthy, hedges need lower-growing plants at their base rather than taller ones that themselves cast shade. *Asplenium trichomanoides* and *A. scolopendrium* both like growing in and at the base of walls, and violets, primroses, snowdrops, crocuses and cyclamen are all suitable species for the base of hedges and fences, as is *Campanula persicifolia*, with its basal leaves and trails of lilac-blue flowers (Lloyd, 2021). The flowers climb into the hedge, but as they are only there for a few weeks they are not a problem.

It is not only the trees, boundaries and screens in a garden that cast shade; when designing overlapping layers of planting to give interest across many months of the year, an understanding of the ways in which one plant shades another is necessary, together with a knowledge of plants that are truly happy in shady conditions. Large-leafed, jungle-like species can erupt from nothing to cast deep shade over a fairly large area. Two such that like moist conditions and look good on the edge of a pond are *Darmera peltata* and *Rodgersia pinnata* 'Superba'. The former has pink flowers in spring before the parasol-shaped leaves emerge – in autumn they turn red – and the latter's plume-like rose-red flowers in summer produce long-lasting seedheads. Snowdrops and crocuses will be happy shaded by these giants as will the spring-flowering anemones, *Anemone blanda* and *A. nemerosa*. *Helleborus foetidus* does not want it too damp but will happily cope with shade, produces pale green flowers in winter and will self-seed around the garden. In my experience *Helleborus orientalis* also copes with being partially shaded and overgrown by other plants in the summer. In autumn its leaves are cut back, allowing space for the winter flower stems. *Pulmonaria officinalis* also survives being shaded later in the year; sometimes the leaves disappear completely in the summer, but it always seems to return in the winter and spring. Some ferns, such as *Polypodium*, are also surprisingly accommodating, coping with dryish shade during the summer months.

Sprays of lilac-blue *Campanula* trail through *Hydrangea* 'Annabelle'.

The flowers of *Darmera peltata* rise up through *Persicaria bistorta* 'Superba' by the water in Beth Chatto's Garden.

Spring

Spring is a time of new beginnings in the garden, when little green shoots start to pop up through the soil and delicate buds unfurl. Bulbs (*see* Chapter 4) provide colour in what is sometimes a drab, grey time of the year and these can be chosen to give waves of interest: snowdrops and crocuses from January onwards, narcissus, then tulips, alliums and more as the season progresses and turns towards summer.

In late February and early March (perhaps this is more correctly still winter) there are the delicate varieties of *Iris reticulata*, which can be planted near the front of the border where their beautiful purple and blue markings can be seen in close up, but they are also a good choice for planting in pots. Try combining them with the Japanese painted fern, *Athyrium niponicum* var. *pictum*. This has soft, bipinnate fronds of greenish grey with hints of silver and dark red (there are also different cultivars, *A. niponicum* var. *pictum* 'Metallicum' and 'Ursula's Red' that have more defined silver and red colouring respectively). The dead leaves of these deciduous ferns can be left to protect the crown in winter and only removed as the irises start to emerge. Soon after the flowers fade tiny fern fronds appear.

The low-growing wood anemone, *Anemone nemorosa*, has deeply cut leaves and pretty white flowers and, as its name suggests, is happy in the shade. After flowering in the spring, it enters a dormant period and disappears before reappearing in the winter. In spring the white variety can bring light to shady areas beneath shrubs and trees, or alternatively there are some with lavender-blue flowers, for example *A. nemorosa* 'Robinsoniana'. Both could be planted with deciduous ferns and grasses that bring interest later in the year. *Viola riviniana*, the dog violet, is also a useful addition to the woodland garden with its purple flowers in late spring. Lloyd (2021) suggests planting it into the crowns of larger perennials, such as *Eupatorium purpureum* 'Atropurpureum', where it will be shaded later in the year when the perennial takes over. Anemones and primroses can also be planted amongst soft fruit, such as blackcurrants and raspberries, to bring spring interest to the more functional areas of the garden.

Blue-flowering bulbs look especially lovely when combined with lime-green flowers. One suggestion is to plant scillas or grape hyacinth or the violet, *Viola labradorica*, with *Euphorbia palustris*. Although the foliage of the *Euphorbia* is not evergreen it does turn yellow

Camassia naturalising in long grass at Markshall in Essex.

and orange in the autumn. A much larger blue-flowering bulb is *Camassia leichtlinii* 'Caerulea' with its dramatic spires of star-shaped flowers and long linear leaves. The bright blue accents repeated around the garden are a delight and they cope well with heavy clay soils, and with sun and semi-shade. They also look wonderful with lime-green – a ground cover of *Heuchera* 'Lime Marmalade' maybe. The leaves of the *Camassia* are prolific and do flop over and take up space in the border but as they die, they still keep their green, rather than quickly turning brown. They can be partially concealed amongst the emerging leaves of deciduous shrubs, but perhaps it is better to place this bulb towards the back of the border or to plant them in long grass.

The dying leaves of all bulbs are a problem for gardeners, especially where space is a premium. Smaller leaved bulbs can be combined with perennials such as *Hemerocallis* that come into leaf early and can help to disguise the dying vegetation; the leaves of the daylily are very similar in texture to those of the bulbs, which also helps. The later-flowering ground cover plant, *Buglossoides purpurocaerulea*, with its gentian-blue flowers in late spring and early summer, also combines well in succession with small bulbs. In a hot, dry position mounds of *Gypsophila* 'Rosenschleier' can also be used to conceal smaller-leafed bulbs; its airy mass allows some light to penetrate to the leaves below. Geraniums, sedums and *Astrantia* start producing leaves early and are useful to plant in combination with some of the later bulbs, such as *Nectaroscordum* and *Allium*.

Spring details (clockwise from top left): *Crocus tommasinianus* 'Whitewell Purple', *Libertia peregrinans*, pots of brightly coloured tulips, *Iris reticulata, Witch hazel,* and *Tellima* and *Ajuga*.

Combination for Semi-Shade

This combination inspired by suggestions from the late Christopher Lloyd (2021), demonstrates how to design for seasonal succession in a small area of the garden that is in semi-shade. The finely cut foliage of the evergreen fern *Polystichum setiferum* Acutilobum Group acts as a foil to a group of white lilies, *Lilium martagon* var. *album,* and a second, taller fern, *Athyrium filix-femina* 'Plumosa Axminster', also with lacy leaves, contrasts with a group of blue-green leaved *Hosta* 'Halcyon'. The latter fern and hostas are both deciduous, but behind them is the evergreen, *Sarcococca ruscifolia,* and nearby a mass of ground cover, *Epimedium* × *perralchicum* 'Fröhnleiten' with its bright yellow spring flowers and evergreen leaves. The yellow flowers of the early *Narcissus* 'February Gold' are dotted in groups through the planting and finally, *Euphorbia amygdaloides* var. *robbiae* 'Atropurpurea' is allowed a limited amount of self-seeding through the scheme, its lime-green flowers contrasting with the darker greens.

There are many shrubs that flower in spring; some of these, however, have one season of interest and therefore it is important to ensure that there are other plants to attract attention through the rest of the year. This is especially true in a small garden where a large shrub can easily dominate the limited space. In the table below I give a few suggestions of what to plant for spring in the garden, but confine myself to those plants that also have a second season of interest.

Contrasting colours of *Euphorbia robbiae* 'Purpurea' and *Helleborus foetidus* bring a splash of drama to the spring scene. (With special thanks to the Provost and Fellows of The Queen's College.)

Table 12 Suggestions for spring leaves and flowers

Plant name	Attributes for the seasonal garden
Shrubs	
Enkianthus campanulatus	Clusters of small cream and red bell-shaped flowers hang from the branches. Leaves turn bright red, orange and yellow in autumn. A good pollinator plant.
Viburnum opulus 'Roseum'	Lovely early foliage and acid-green fluffy flowers that turn white as they age. Leaves turn a reddish colour in autumn. This variety is sterile so does not have berries. For wildlife and berries choose the native *Viburnum opulus*.
Viburnum plicatum f. *tomentosum* 'Mariesii'	A large shrub with a distinctive horizontal layered habit, white lacecap flowers and purple autumn colour.
Climbers and wall shrubs	
Chaenomeles species in red, white, peach and pink	These wall shrubs flower profusely on their bare branches from winter through spring for several months. They also cope with semi-shade. Some species hug the ground, others are more vertical in their habit. The flowers are followed by yellowish quince-like fruits.
Clematis armandii 'Apple Blossom'	Gloriously scented, creamy-coloured flowers and evergreen leaves. But be careful as this clematis can take over.
Perennials	
Ajuga reptans 'Catlin's Giant'	Evergreen purple-green leaves, larger than other ajugas, and blue flowers held above the leaves throughout late spring and early summer.
Brunnera macrophylla 'Jack Frost'	Large, heart-shaped silver leaves with green veining create a bright ground cover in shade. Small blue flowers held above leaves in spring. The foliage dies back in late summer but would look good planted with *Ajuga*.
Cynara cardunculus	This statuesque cardoon is attractive to pollinators and is an asset throughout the year, but in spring its dead seedheads are still standing, creating a dramatic accent and the silver leaves are already making a bold statement.
Pulmonaria longifolia	Blue spring flowers and long, narrow, semi-evergreen leaves with white blotches, for shade under trees.

Enkianthus campanulatus flowers from late spring into the summer, seen here in Beth Chatto's woodland garden catching the dappled light. The wood is underplanted with spring bulbs and then the bright yellow daisy-like flowers of *Doronicum pardalianches* take over.

Mediterranean Growing Period

Rather than spring and summer, the growing season for many Mediterranean plants is during the cooler and wetter months of winter and spring; in this way they avoid being stressed in summer droughts. Some species can become dormant when necessary – they should be thought of as avoiding drought rather than tolerating it (Hitchmough, 1994). Examples include *Acanthus spinosus* and *Oenothera lindheimeri* (formerly *Gaura*).

There are other species that flower in early summer, but they will then rest and do not even require any watering. In fact, some, such as *Arum italicum* subsp. 'Marmoratum' and *Cyclamen hederifolium* disappear altogether. The *Arum* has a display of handsome silver veined leaves that grow through the winter. The greenish-yellow spathes appear and the leaves die back and then in autumn, a spire of bright orange-red berries appears. These plants grow in semi-shade and therefore

A flowering *Ferula* is the dramatic centrepiece of this planting scheme at Beth Chatto's Garden. It is surrounded by forget-me-nots and *Allium* 'Purple Rain'.

are happy under shrubs and trees or combined with ferns and hostas. There are also two hardy geraniums that behave in this way, forming leaves in winter and early spring, flowering in spring, putting on lots of leaf growth and dying back in summer: *Geranium malviflorum* has purple-blue flowers with red veining and *G. tuberosum* is a paler pinkish purple. Both are attractive to pollinators and would be suitable to plant in a sunny space that is taken over by a taller species later in the year.

Ferula communis, a giant fennel, is another Mediterranean species that grows in the cooler seasons, its filigree leaves appearing in the winter and dying back in the summer; it may also die completely after flowering and setting seed. It does not flower on an annual basis and may only build up the strength to create its magnificent dramatic flower head once every two or three years (Lloyd, 2021) (Pearson, 2018). When this happens there is the sculptural skeleton structure of seedheads and stems to look forward to, but to keep a reliable interest through the summer interplant the *Ferula* with tall annuals (*see* Chapter 4), or plant it in combination with *Cistus* or with *Phlomis* 'Edward Bowles' and mid-height grasses such as *Panicum virgatum* 'Warrior' or *Molinia* 'Heidebraut'.

Although an understanding of the summer dormant period may prove useful when choosing plants to cope with the changing climate, it is important to remember that the UK differs from the Mediterranean in several respects. For any plant the growing season is dependent on the degree of shade, daylight hours, moisture and temperature and these factors vary with the weather conditions, and with factors such as latitude and cloud cover. To illustrate this, James Hitchmough gives the example of *Iris unguicularis* that grows in dense shade in the Mediterranean, but in the UK it needs to be planted in the sun in order to flower (Hitchmough, 1994). This is because the strength of the sun's rays in the UK's northern latitude is not as great as in the Mediterranean.

Summer

Summer is the easiest season when thinking about the successional garden and I have already included many design ideas and plant choices in earlier chapters. In Chapter 4 I discussed how to layer species in a scheme from early flowering bulbs and ground cover through to the later-flowering perennials and grasses, and I also included a section on growing from seed. Here I look at some special cases as well as discussing how to extend the flowering period.

Extending the Flowering Period

Some plants just keep on flowering for months with little encouragement. Although it is always exciting to have a diverse range of flowers popping up at different times, choosing some with a long flowering season can ensure you have a backdrop of colour through the summer and into the autumn, although these species usually have little or no winter interest. The perennial wallflower, *Erysimum* 'Bowles's Mauve', flowers from March right through the summer and, although it is sterile, it still produces nectar and is attractive to bees. There are many geraniums that also have this attribute: one that is loved by solitary bees is the blue-flowered *Geranium* 'Rozanne' (Rollings, 2019). For magenta flowers try *G.* 'Dragon Heart' or *G.* 'Light Dilys' with pink flowers veined in red. Apricot coloured *Geum* 'Mai Tai' and the bright orange *G.* 'Totally Tangerine' both have a long season from late spring into the summer and if you have a well-drained soil, salvias are a great choice with their many shades of purple and pink. Shrubby potentillas flower from summer into late autumn, creating low mounds in the middle and to the front of the border. Examples include *Potentilla fruticosa* 'Marian Red Robin' and the earlier flowering *P. fruticosa* 'Primrose Beauty' with its silky grey-green leaves. Both are attractive to pollinators.

It is not only roses that can be deadheaded to encourage repeat flowering; there are many perennials that benefit from this intervention. It is also possible to cut back some species to just above ground level to encourage new young leaf growth and sometimes a second flush of flowers (*see* Chapter 8 for information about the 'Chelsea Chop'). Deadheading prevents the plant setting seed and so is not suitable for those species that you are relying on to provide autumn and winter seedheads. Similarly, roses that produce attractive hips should not be deadheaded. Hardy geraniums, delphiniums and lupins are three species that can be cut back after flowering and may then produce new growth and flowers. *Nepeta* 'Six Hills Giant' starts flowering in May and can be cut back in July, after which it will produce leaves and another flush of flowers that last well into the autumn (Crocus, n.d.). *Alchemilla mollis* and *Astrantia* also produce new soft green foliage after cutting back.

The orange-red *Helenium* 'Moerheim Beauty' can be deadheaded from the middle of July into August to extend the flowering season. Similarly, *Helenium* 'Sahin's Early Flowerer' responds well to deadheading and, because it is a great pollinator plant, this also benefits wildlife (Rollings, 2019). This latter *Helenium* is useful as it fills what is sometimes known as the 'June Gap' – a period when there are fewer pollinator-friendly species in flower (Rollings, 2018). Another species that is good for pollinators is *Phlox paniculata* 'Blue Paradise', which flowers from June to September if it is deadheaded. Then there are varieties of penstemon, geum, dahlias and many more (*Gardeners' World*, 2021).

Long Sunny Border with Yew Buttresses

One of designer Philippa O'Brien's aims when planning this colourful border in full sun was to ensure that there were flowers for as long as possible through the spring, summer and autumn. The colour palette is dramatic, consisting of many shades of pink and purple with some whites and the deep pink of the repeat-flowering *Rosa* 'Gertrude Jekyll'. Bold clipped yew buttresses divide the bed and provide a winter backdrop to the dead flower heads of *Calamagrostis* × *acutiflora* 'Karl Foerster' and *Eupatorium* 'Riesenschirm'. The soft feathery *Nassella tenuissima* (otherwise known as *Stipa tenuissima*) flows over onto the path at the front, also bringing winter interest, and there are bulbs to fill the period before the perennials take over. But it is the choice of species known for their long flowering period that ensures this design has interest throughout the year: *Salvia* 'Caradonna', *S.* 'Nachtvlinder', *S.* Neon and *S.* 'Amistad' (not usually hardy) all flower for long periods, especially if they are deadheaded, and *Phlox paniculata* 'Starfire' and *Eurybia divaricata* also put on a good show from summer into autumn. Apparently Gertrude Jekyll used to plant *Eurybia divaricata* in semi-shade amongst *Bergenia*, the latter helping to support the thin black stems with their frothy flowers (Beth Chatto's plants and gardens, n.d.).

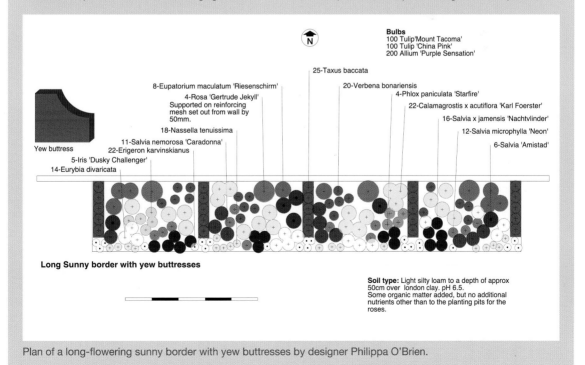

Long Sunny border with yew buttresses

Plan of a long-flowering sunny border with yew buttresses by designer Philippa O'Brien.

Long-flowering salvias contrast with *Phlomis russeliana*. A clipped yew adds year-round drama and structure in a design at Kew Gardens by Richard Wildford.

Climbers

Most climbers tend to grow vigorously once established and are useful to cover fences and sheds, but may leave bare gaps in winter when they lose their leaves or have to be cut back. Often the straggling stems are unattractive and therefore introducing pergolas, obelisks and ornate screens is a good way of ensuring there is an attractive structural presence in the dormant season, but it is important to match the vigour of the climber to the support. It is sometimes suggested that planting a climber to scramble through a tree is a good way to add seasonal interest to a design. However, in the case of many vigorous climbing species, this can result in the form of the tree being concealed, leaving little more than a tall blob of vegetation for much of the year and therefore the choice of climber needs to be carefully considered.

Table 13 Useful climbers for successional schemes

Climber/wall shrub	Attributes for seasonal succession
Akebia quinata	Clusters of hanging spring flowers, beautifully scented, and bright green leaves that usually last through the winter. The chocolatey-maroon flowers look lovely in combination with lime green.
Celastrus orbiculatus	This is a fast-growing deciduous vine with inconspicuous greenish flowers in summer. Its fruit are yellow and sometimes split to reveal scarlet-red seeds. Make sure you choose the hermaphrodite form in order to get fruit from a single plant.
Clematis 'Etoile Violette' and *C.* 'Purpurea Plena Elegans'	These late-flowering clematis can be planted to scramble through evergreen shrubs to add to the seasons of interest (Thomas, 2008).
Clematis tangutica 'Little Lemons'	Nodding lemon-coloured flowers from June onwards followed by fluffy seedheads that last well into the winter.
Garrya elliptica 'James Roof'	Long, grey catkins gradually extend into silvery tassels up to 20cm long. Use as a large wall shrub and place where the catkins can be seen to good effect. But remember that when there are no catkins there need to be some other plants nearby to catch the interest.
Hedera helix 'Parsley Crested'	There are many textural ivies with interesting leaves. This one has bright green leaves with crinkled edges.
Itea ilicifolia	*Itea* can be trained as a wall shrub. It has evergreen, holly-like leaves and long racemes of green-white flowers in summer and autumn with a honey scent. Hilary Thomas (2008) suggests growing it with the contrasting leaves of *Vitis vinifera* 'Purpurea' (if you have plenty of space).
Trachylospermum jasminoides	Every garden should have a *Trachylospermum* with its glossy evergreen leaves and scented white flowers for weeks over the summer.
Wisteria sinensis 'Amethyst'	Wonderfully scented mauve flowers before the leaves appear. Some wisteria keep their unusual hanging seed pods through the winter.

Self-seeders, climbers and wall shrubs in summer (clockwise from top left): trailing *Clematis* 'Betty Corning', *Cytisus battandieri* trained on wall, *Aqueligia canadensis* self-seeding along the path, a delicate single-flowered rose climbs through an *Elaeagnus angustifolia*, foxglove and *Cercis* 'Forest Pansy', fennel and poppies self-seeding among daylilies.

Self-Seeders and Ephemeral Perennials

Allowing perennials and grasses to set seed and disperse freely around the garden can contribute to the diversity of planting, but there is always a danger that opportunist species begin to dominate. It is also not always easy to predict which plants will be happy self-seeding and which will not: in fact, each year may produce different results. However, an element of chance adds surprise to the planting design; dots of bright colour sprinkled amongst other more static plants can even unify a scheme and ephemeral species add to the atmosphere of the garden. The table below makes a few suggestions for species that make useful additions to the successional garden palette.

Table 14 Suggestions for perennials and grasses that may self-seed

Self-seeder	Comments
Alchemilla mollis	Textural leaves and lime-green flowers, but be prepared to weed out undesirable seedlings. Can be cut back after flowering to encourage new growth.
Astrantia major 'Alba' Astrantia 'Claret	A white and a red Astrantia, both produce masses of flowers, can be cut back for new growth and sometimes an extra flush of flowers and will self-seed in a well-behaved fashion. They cope with semi-shade.
Digitalis purpurea and cultivars	Accent plants with spires that rise above other perennials that are yet to be in full bloom. Thought of as shade loving but do need some light, so are best in semi-shade.
Eryngium giganteum	Known as Miss Willmott's Ghost (apparently, she used to scatter seeds in the gardens she visited) this short-lived, statuesque Eryngium has silver-grey bracts and blueish flowers. It is a good species for pollinators.
Foeniculum vulgare	Feathery leaves, greenish-yellow flowers. Wonderful skeleton stems and seedheads last through the winter.
Lunaria annua	The annual honesty has lovely seedheads as well as purple flowers. Copes with dry shade so combines well with deciduous ferns.
Myosotis sylvatica	Forget-me-nots are good plants for pollinators, usually biennial. They only have one season of interest but are easy to pull up if unwanted and create a pretty, low, frothy mass of blue around the base of taller growing perennials or amongst other ground cover.
Nassella tenuissima (Stipa tenuissima)	A delicate, feathery fountain of grass and flower heads.

Combination for Full Sun

This combination is inspired by some of the plants in the late Beth Chatto's gravel garden (1978). Cercis siliquastrum forms the backdrop to the group. It is a wonderful tree for a seasonal garden and for pollinators, with its clusters of early, bright pink flowers on bare branches, bronze new leaves and purple seed pods. Spring-flowering Euphorbia characias subsp. wulfenii adds height behind a variety of evergreen silver-leafed species that cope with dry conditions, including Ruta graveolens 'Jackman's Blue' and Santolina incana, both of which can be trimmed in summer to encourage new growth. Dot the pale purple globes of Allium christophii through the silver-blue foliage and allow Lychnis coronaria with its magenta flowers, to self-seed. Allium carinatum subsp. pulchellum can be dotted around for interest later in the summer. To relieve the silver-grey colour palette, add two hebes: Hebe 'Autumn Glory' and the smaller ground cover, Hebe 'Carl Teschner'. And for a spiky presence to contrast with the low domes, try Iris pallida 'Argentea Variegata' with pale purple flowers and variegated foliage.

Autumn

Many of the plants discussed in this book have flowering periods that extend into the autumn, and I have touched on the importance of appreciating dead and dying forms to add interest in the later months of the year. Some species die more gracefully than others and there are those that produce dramatic winter skeletons of stems and seedheads. These are rarely colourful, comprised as they are of greys and browns, although, especially in the case of grasses, we can find rusts and sometimes golds – the latter especially when seen in low sunlight.

However, autumn has its own dramatic displays of colour as leaves gradually change and die, and berries and fruits develop. There are also the delicate pinks and purples of cyclamens and colchicums emerging at the base of shrubs and trees. The following table gives just a few suggestions for autumn planting, including late-flowering species and those with good autumn colour or berries.

A front garden in autumn enlivened with frames of box hedging, and the dead flower and seedheads of *Hydrangea* 'Annabelle' and *Calamagrostis* 'Overdam'.

Autumn details (clockwise from top left): Two contrasting acers, bright pink *Nerine* among wispy grasses, dead flower heads of *Achillea*, leaves of *Cercis* 'Forest Pansy', dead seedheads of *Ceratostigma willmottianum*, berries of *Viburnum opulus*.

A view of an urban garden in autumn, design by the author.

Table 15 A selection of plants for autumn colour and berries

Tree/shrub	Attributes for seasonal succession
Acer shirasawanum 'Aureum'	There are so many acers to choose from for autumn colour, but this one has buttery-yellow leaves in spring and summer, little red flowers in spring and red autumn colouring.
Berberis wilsoniae	Pale yellow spring flowers and grey-green leaves that turn red and orange in autumn together with translucent pink berries.
Ceratostigma plumbaginoides	A low-growing choice for the front of the border with vivid blue flowers in late summer and bright red leaves in autumn. Plant with *Euphorbia rigida* for winter and spring interest.
Ceratostigma willmottianum	Cobalt-blue flowers for a long period over the summer and into autumn. Russet-red leaves in autumn. Unusual spiky seedheads that last through the winter. A low spreading shrub that forms a mound near the front of a border. The branches arch gracefully over paths. Can be underplanted with early bulbs.
Cercis canadensis 'Forest Pansy'	Heart-shaped purple leaves that change to orange, bronze and red in autumn. Looks wonderful when backlit.
Cotoneaster 'Rothschildianus'	A semi-evergreen shrub with willow-like leaves and creamy-white flowers followed by yellow berries. Suitable for north- and east-facing walls.
Crataegus × prunifolia 'Splendens'	This hawthorn has white flowers, red berries and red and orange autumn colour.
Malus 'Evereste'	Masses of white flowers in spring, yellow leaf colour in autumn and red-orange crab apples that are loved by the birds.
Sorbus vilmorinii	This small tree has creamy white flowers and pinkish-white berries as well as purple autumn leaf colour.
Vaccinium corymbosum 'Collins'	Blueberries need acid soil and are a great plant for pots. Many, including this variety, have wonderful red autumn colour as well as pretty creamy-bronze flowers and edible fruits.

Long-Lasting Seedheads

Dan Pearson's planting schemes at a development around King's Cross in London are inspirational examples of how to create interest and enjoyment throughout the year. The photos were taken in February after a winter that included ten days of ice and snow cover as well as high rainfall. Many plants were still standing tall, catching the low sunlight on their brown and golden stems.

Evergreens include low clipped hedges of mixed box and yew, as well as mounds of felty-grey *Ballota pseudodictamnus* and the fountain stems of species of South African restio. Deciduous multi-stemmed trees, such as varieties of hawthorn, give structure to the winter scene and the stems of *Hamamelis* are already covered in red and yellow spidery flowers.

Giant perennials that have kept their dead flower and seedheads include: *Eryngium pandanifolium* 'Physic Purple' that has reddish-purple cone-like flowers on branched stems in late summer; *Vernonia arkansana*, also late flowering with clusters of purple daisy-like flowers held high on stiff stems; *Datisca cannabina* with huge mounds of pinnate foliage in spring and tall arching stems of greenish-white flower fringes in late summer, and also *Baptisia australis* 'Purple Smoke' (smaller than the three giants) with purple pea-like flowers in early summer and dark seed pods. Adding a solid vertical presence to the more informal seedheads are blocks of grasses including *Miscanthus* and *Calamagrostis*.

In spring the bright new foliage of the perennials is dotted with alliums and later in the year there will be many other species to bring colour to the scheme, including various varieties of *Sanguisorba*, *Persicaria* and Japanese anemone.

Eryngium pandanifolium 'Physic Purple' in a planting design by Dan Pearson.

The giant dead stems of *Datisca cannabina* in a planting design by Dan Pearson.

Black seedheads of *Baptisia australis* 'Purple Smoke' spill over the paving in a planting design by Dan Pearson.

CHAPTER 6

PLANTING IN MINERAL SUBSTRATES

Expedience, a desire for sustainability and requirements of longevity and low maintenance are often behind the choice of planting design approach, but there is no reason such schemes cannot also provide atmosphere, changing colours and drama throughout the year. Many of the gardens discussed in this book consider all these factors; however, there is growing interest in creating gardens in which sustainability and resilience are a priority. Designers and gardeners are experimenting with schemes in places where there is no usable topsoil or where materials found on site and locally are used to create growing substrates. In this chapter we will look at gardens grown on mineral mulches and those designed for sites in the Mediterranean that are often created on rocky, infertile sites and that have to take account of a summer dormant period – something that may become more important for UK gardeners as the climate crisis progresses.

However, many gardens will already have perfectly workable topsoil on site and therefore I start this chapter with a brief section discussing types of soils and introducing the 'no-dig' approach to gardening.

Soil and Substrates

Understanding the soil you have to work with is an essential first step to choosing a plant palette for a garden. There are six basic types: clay, silt, sand, loam, chalk (highly alkaline) and peat (rarely found in gardens). It is the size of the main particles that gives soil its characteristics and helps to determine what can successfully be grown. Clay soils, which have small particles, can be very fertile and hold water, taking a long time to drain. They are also easily compacted in the wet winter months and can harden and crack like concrete in hot summers. Conversely, sandy soils are well-drained but lack nutrients, which are quickly washed away. Gardening books talk of creating beds that consist of a fine loam – a mix of clay and sand plus some silt. This can take years of work, of improving the soil, adding organic matter and mulching, but any soil can benefit from the addition of manures, composts and the planting of green manures that not only improve the structure, but also release nutrients slowly over time. The pH is also important, but most plants will grow in soils that are neutral or tend towards either acidic or alkaline – although there are exceptions, including the acid-loving heathers, rhododendrons and azaleas.

A focus on sustainability means that working with what is on site is the best solution. Include a compost heap and space to produce leaf mould wherever possible and set expectations with the garden owner from the outset. Mulching plants in the autumn or early spring helps to improve the soil and allows plants to thrive. All these aspects of soil care apply to any garden; however, in order to get the best from a seasonal successional garden, it is necessary to understand how soil fertility affects growth. Obviously, it is important to ensure there are sufficient nutrients for flowering, setting seed and surviving into the next year. However, in fertile soils, a plant can grow lanky and soft, resulting in a need for staking to ensure it does not collapse and swamp the lower-growing, early-flowering species close by. This excessive growth also applies to some perennials if they are overcrowded; perhaps they need to be divided or will not be happy in competition with other plants.

As we will explore in the remainder of this chapter, it is possible to reuse hard landscaping materials to modify the substrates in a garden, allowing you to plant a diverse range of species that might otherwise not be possible. John Little's (Bower, 2021) research (*see* below) has shown that a good-quality topsoil is not necessarily a requirement for plant growth. This is seen in practice where brownfield sites are left untouched and fall into dereliction, and yet opportunist and specialist species begin to colonise the, often contaminated, open spaces.

The No-Dig Gardening System

The no-dig method of gardening is advocated by Charles Dowding (2018) for use when growing vegetables, but there is no reason why it should not be modified to apply to other more ornamental gardens as well, particularly where organic gardening methods are practised. The structure of soils is easily destroyed through digging and breaking up the ground and, by reducing or eliminating this, the microorganisms, fungi, worms and structure of the soil itself can be protected. It is important to eliminate weeds prior to planting and this can be done by laying a light-excluding material – preferably not a landscape fabric, cardboard can work just as well and eventually rots down into the soil (*Garden Organic*, 2021). Compost or other organic matter is laid on top of the cardboard in a thick layer, around 15–20cm to start with, and the weeds that are starved of light eventually die. There may be some more pernicious species that have to be dug out individually by hand, but the idea is that as time progresses, small weed seedlings can easily be hoed from the top layer of compost.

When it comes to planting, if you are using plugs or small 9cm and 1 litre pots then the little plants can just be popped straight into the compost layer without disturbing the soil. Obviously, holes will need to be dug for the more mature species and it is probably better to plant any specimen trees and shrubs before applying the compost layer. The no-dig method is particularly useful for planting annuals, either as seeds or as seedlings.

Industrial Wastelands and Succession

Brownfield sites and industrial wastelands are often perceived as a blight on the area, as places merely awaiting development (English Partnerships, 2006). However, these places often have value for local people, sometimes through the memories they evoke (Heatherington, 2018) and also through the opportunities they offer for experiencing nature in an urban environment (Heatherington et al., 2017) (Heatherington, 2012). There is a growing understanding that such sites enable unusual and varied habitats to develop on the waste substrates left behind after industries have closed. These habitats, known as Open Mosaic Habitats, may be contaminated, but can still support a diverse range of pioneer species and invertebrates (Buglife, n.d.).

The ways in which species colonise brownfield sites has led some designers and gardeners to experiment with different substrates in their own gardens and landscapes. It is worth noting that it is not only native plants that thrive on these sorts of sites; the varied substrates can support unusual non-native species and can therefore be a way to introduce colourful flowers both early and late in the season. However, introducing thick layers of virgin mineral aggregate, as in some of the case studies below, is not necessarily a sustainable approach and using reclaimed and

Top left: A Berlin signal box in an abandoned site where an Open Mosaic Habitat is establishing. Top right: In Berlin, the nature reserve of Südgelände was abandoned for decades. Traces of its history remain in the forms of the ghostly remnants of railway tracks running through the vegetation.

recycled substrates, sometimes in combination with gravel, may be a better solution in certain situations (Bower, 2021).

Growing on Reclaimed Substrates – John Little

For over 25 years John Little has been experimenting with plantings on reclaimed substrates such as crushed glass, sand, concrete and even coal and crushed ceramic toilets. At his garden in Essex (the image at the beginning of this chapter shows his garden in summer) he has removed most of the topsoil, reusing it in a vegetable garden, and created around twenty different habitats on a wide range of substrates that vary in depth from 100–500mm thus forming an undulating ground plane interspersed with mounds. For those who are interested, more information on the different types of substrate can be found in Sally Bower's informative report for the RHS (2021). When I met with

Little, he showed me the difference between a seed mix grown on rubble laid on the topsoil and the same mix grown in an area where the topsoil was removed before the addition of a layer of rubble. It was clear that the latter supported a much more diverse range of species because the fertility was low, and thus competition was less of an issue. Where there was topsoil beneath the rubble, fertility was increased with the result that the plants grew taller, and it was also noticeable that the diversity was reduced.

In places where perennial weeds are a problem Little uses a geotextile membrane below the mineral layer, but he cautions that this type of gardening cannot be described as low maintenance and there is always a need to be vigilant, removing weeds when they are small. All the plants have been grown from seed, both native and non-native, with no addition of fertilisers. Keeping the fertility low can help to ensure that weeds are less of a problem and by using seeds rather than plastic pots and compost he is also

Gabion walls give structure in John Little's garden in Essex.

reducing the carbon footprint of his garden (Westhorpe, 2021). Little was originally inspired by the Open Mosaic Habitats found on brownfield sites and the diversity of habitats and the addition of structural elements, such as ponds and log piles in the garden support a wide range of invertebrates in much the same way as brownfield landscapes. The resulting garden is informal and naturalistic with many species that self-seed, including *Oenothera* 'Lemon Sunset', *Echium vulgare*, *Lathyrus latifolius*, *Foeniculum vulgare* and *Daucus carota* (Westhorpe, 2021). He also includes a few pot-grown, non-native species such as the ground cover *Symphyotrichum ericoides* var. *prostratum* 'Snow Flurry' which has a mass of white autumn flowers and purple-flowering *Salvia* 'Allen Chickering' (Hunt, 2023).

The range of different substrates and plants support a huge diversity of invertebrates. Just one example is the native climber, white bryony, *Bryonia dioica*, that is the sole food source for the bryony mining bee. This bee also needs sandy soil to build nest burrows; once Little planted the bryony, the bees arrived to take advantage of both the food supply and the habitat. White bryony is a vigorous climber with lobed leaves that flowers from May to August and also has bright red berries, but be careful as it is toxic to humans and cattle.

Little has introduced other interventions for wildlife such as timber posts, wood piles and gabions and these, together with the trees that punctuate the ground plane and frame the mass of vegetation, all help to provide structural and seasonal interest. A recent favourite tree (Hunt, 2023) is the vase-shaped *Heptacodium miconioides*, known as the seven son flower, which has panicles of white star-shaped flowers in September and peeling yellowish-brown bark. The calyx of the flowers extends and turns a purple red after flowering.

However, there are few shrubs to add winter interest and, apart from the anchoring elements of the trees and dead logs, interest during the dormant periods comes from the colours and textures of the different substrates as well as the dying seedheads. Little

Above: Verbascum seedheads still standing after the winter, echo the verticals of the dead logs and provide yet another habitat in John Little's garden. Left: A close-up of the decorative hanging seedheads of woad, *Isatis tinctora*, in John Little's garden.

suggests a few species that stand through the winter. These include species of *Achillea*, teasel, the sub-shrub spiny restharrow (*Ononis spinosa*), fennel and *Ferula*. He also has several varieties of verbascum including non-native *Verbascum blattaria*, the moth mullein, and native *V. nigrum*, the dark mullein. The seedheads of these are left standing into the spring and mingle with a cluster of upright gnarled dead tree trunks, which form yet another habitat. Although unconventional, Little's way of gardening does provide interest and drama through the seasons and the masses and voids, atmosphere, colours and textures wax and wane as the year progresses. One tip that he gives to ensure different flowering periods is to mow/cut back sections of the vegetation at different times; this results in some species flowering later than normal (and they may not be so tall), adding to the dynamism of the planting.

Using a Mineral Substrate and Mulch

As illustrated in John Little's garden above, all manner of materials can be used as a mineral substrate or mulch; the main factor is that they do not contain organic matter. Other things to consider when designing these types of gardens are the source of the materials, the depth of substrate, the diameter of the materials and whether fines (finely crushed dust-like particles) are incorporated. In the next sections I look at several gardens created using mineral mulches and substrates and discuss the management implications; and in Chapter 7, I discuss the benefits for wildlife in the walled garden at Knepp Castle Estate, also designed using recycled substrates and shown in photos here.

Echinacea pallida ripples through the walled garden created from reclaimed substrates on the Knepp Castle Estate, designed by Tom Stuart-Smith and James Hitchmough.

Reducing Weed Germination

Recent research by Hitchmough and Livingstone (2020) of the University of Sheffield examines the suitability of using deep mineral mulches as a planting medium. Their aim was to monitor the establishment and growth of different plant species and the effect that a mineral mulch had on wind-blown weed germination. The mulches were laid to a depth of 150-200mm with the most successful being fines-free, pea gravel, 4–10mm diameter. Such mulches have little water-holding capacity and therefore wind-blown weeds find it difficult to establish. The perennials and grasses, however, can thrive because there is less competition and eventually their roots penetrate the gravel to obtain water from the soil below. With the right choice of drought and stress-tolerant species, these plantings need no irrigation and can be relatively low maintenance due to the reduction in the need to weed.

Asclepias tuberosa and *Melica ciliata* interlacing in the walled garden at Knepp designed by Tom Stuart-Smith and James Hitchmough.

The Grasslands Garden – James Hitchmough and Wes Shaw

The Grasslands Garden at the Horniman Museum in London was designed by James Hitchmough with the then-head gardener, Wes Shaw, and opened to the public in 2017. The site was dry and fertile heavy clay; 150mm of topsoil was removed as part of the construction of the garden and replaced with 150mm of 10mm pea gravel, providing a sterile substrate for planting that is intended to reduce weed growth (Hitchmough and Livingstone, 2020). Using substrates with no fines also suppresses wind-blown weed germination.

Hitchmough has created two areas of drought-tolerant planting within the site, one imitating a North American prairie and the other a central South African grassland and steppe. The plants, in 9cm pots, are set out at random at 30cm centres, following an interlacing approach (Bower, 2021). Before planting, the top layer of growing medium is removed from each pot to reduce any introduction of weeds and to allow the mineral mulch to be brought up to the stem of the plant. In the table that follows, I have detailed some of the species found in the Grasslands Garden and considered how they could be used in a scheme that follows the warp and weft approach.

Echinacea paradoxa and the fluffy seedheads of *Pulsatilla* at the Grasslands Garden.

Table 16 Sally Bower (2021) and Damien Midgley (2018) highlight some of the species found in the Grasslands Garden

Plant	Warp and weft suggestions	Seasonal interest
North American prairie		
Asclepias tuberosa	Could use for seasonal punctuation in the warp.	Dramatic orange-red flowers from midsummer into autumn.
Baptisia australis	Use as clusters.	A lupin-like plant, which prefers lime-free soil. Spires of rich blue flowers in summer and bold clusters of black swollen seed pods on dark, stiffly upright stems in autumn.
Echinacea paradoxa E. pallida E. tennesseensis 'Rocky Top'	Use as clusters or ripples in the weft.	Yellow and pink varieties of coneflower bring colour through the summer and bobble-like cones remain in the autumn.
Liatris aspera	Use in clusters or as a seasonal accent plant.	Dramatic spires of large purple-pink flowers in summer. Attracts butterflies, bees and parasitic wasps.
Schizachyrium scoparium	Ripple or dot through other lower-growing perennials.	Blue-green foliage and wonderful coppery-orange autumn colour.
South African grassland and steppe		
Berkheya purpurea	Use in clusters or dotted through other lower-growing perennials and grasses.	Forms a small, silvery rosette over winter. Spiky, jagged leaves and lilac-purple flowers all summer.
Bulbinella eburniflora	Accent and punctuation plants.	Striking white or yellow flowers in the summer, held above narrow leaves.
Dierama pulcherrimum	Seasonal punctuation and accents.	Strappy leaves and tall arching stems with dainty bell-like flowers in summer. Looks lovely beside water.
Gladiolus papilio	Clusters or dotted in grasses.	Narrow grey-green leaves and arching flower stems flushed with white and purple throughout the summer and into the autumn.
Hesperantha coccinea	Clusters or dotted.	Grassy leaves and then red flowers throughout the autumn and even into winter if mild.
Kniphofia uvaria	Accent and punctuation plants.	Red-hot pokers have a long flowering period and also are very long-lived.

Growing in Builder's Rubble and Gravel

Rachel Bailey's Design for a Naturalistic Coastal Garden in West Scotland

This coastal garden was designed to link the house and garden with the wider landscape – both visually and functionally – so that it would offer a natural progression beyond the boundaries, act as a corridor for wildlife passing through, and offer year-round interest for those living there.

The topography of the ground was changed from a uniform slope to create gentle mounds. Rocks ranging in size were also nestled into the landscape. Paths meander through the garden mirroring the rolling mountains and the ebbing and flowing of the sea, whilst the planting is inspired by the forms, style and subdued tones of the mountains, moors and coastline of the west of Scotland. Together an Open Mosaic Habitat was formed.

Due to its location, the garden is exposed to south-westerly winds, full sun and wet winters. The open area of the garden also had the added challenge of the rubble from a demolished building being buried there. This resulted in a relatively free-draining, nutrient-poor,

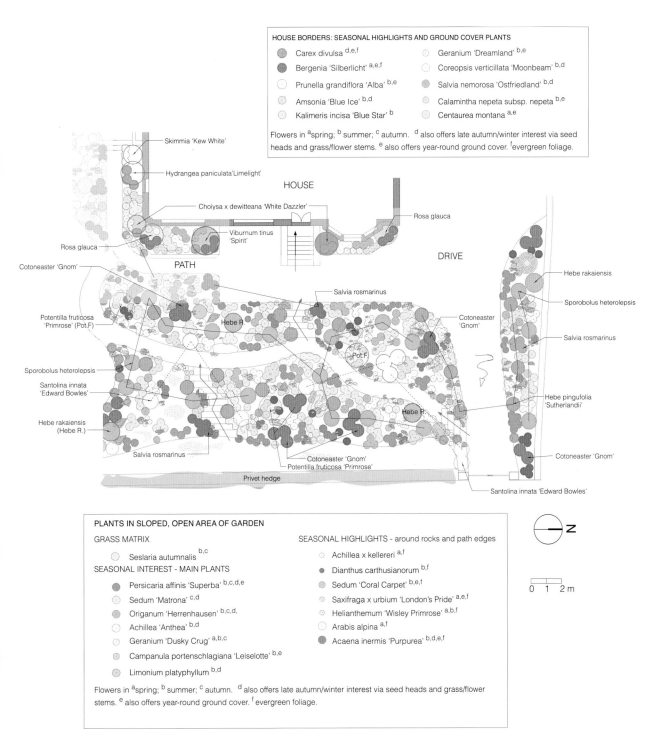

HOUSE BORDERS: SEASONAL HIGHLIGHTS AND GROUND COVER PLANTS

- Carex divulsa [d,e,f]
- Bergenia 'Silberlicht' [a,e,f]
- Prunella grandiflora 'Alba' [b,e]
- Amsonia 'Blue Ice' [b,d]
- Kalimeris incisa 'Blue Star' [b]
- Geranium 'Dreamland' [b,e]
- Coreopsis verticillata 'Moonbeam' [b,d]
- Salvia nemorosa 'Ostfriedland' [b,d]
- Calamintha nepeta subsp. nepeta [b,e]
- Centaurea montana [a,e]

Flowers in [a]spring; [b] summer; [c] autumn. [d] also offers late autumn/winter interest via seed heads and grass/flower stems. [e] also offers year-round ground cover. [f] evergreen foliage.

Skimmia 'Kew White'
Hydrangea paniculata 'Limelight'
HOUSE
Choiysa x dewitteana 'White Dazzler'
Rosa glauca
Viburnum tinus 'Spirit'
Rosa glauca
Cotoneaster 'Gnom'
DRIVE
PATH
Potentilla fruticosa 'Primrose' (Pot.F)
Salvia rosmarinus
Hebe R.
Cotoneaster 'Gnom'
Hebe rakaiensis
Sporobolus heterolepsis
Pot.F
Salvia rosmarinus
Sporobolus heterolepsis
Santolina innata 'Edward Bowles'
Hebe rakaiensis (Hebe R.)
Hebe R.
Hebe pingufolia 'Sutherlandii'
Salvia rosmarinus
Cotoneaster 'Gnom'
Potentilla fruticosa 'Primrose'
Cotoneaster 'Gnom'
Privet hedge
Santolina innata 'Edward Bowles'

N

0 1 2 m

PLANTS IN SLOPED, OPEN AREA OF GARDEN

GRASS MATRIX
- Seslaria autumnalis [b,c]

SEASONAL INTEREST - MAIN PLANTS
- Persicaria affinis 'Superba' [b,c,d,e]
- Sedum 'Matrona' [c,d]
- Origanum 'Herrenhausen' [b,c,d,]
- Achillea 'Anthea' [b,d]
- Geranium 'Dusky Crug' [a,b,c]
- Campanula portenschlagiana 'Leiselotte' [b,e]
- Limonium platyphyllum [b,d]

SEASONAL HIGHLIGHTS - around rocks and path edges
- Achillea x kellereri [a,f]
- Dianthus carthusianorum [b,f]
- Sedum 'Coral Carpet' [b,e,f]
- Saxifraga x urbium 'London's Pride' [a,e,f]
- Helianthemum 'Wisley Primrose' [a,b,f]
- Arabis alpina [a,f]
- Acaena inermis 'Purpurea' [b,d,e,f]

Flowers in [a]spring; [b] summer; [c] autumn. [d] also offers late autumn/winter interest via seed heads and grass/flower stems. [e] also offers year-round ground cover. [f] evergreen foliage.

Plan of Rachel Bailey's naturalistic coastal garden.

alkaline 'soil', much in contrast to the surrounding hills, resembling more the shoreline. This 'substrate' was kept and worked with as an opportunity, turning it into a positive.

Plants were carefully selected by first looking at the natural habitats of species – both native and non-natives, so that they would thrive in the prevailing conditions – the 'soil', exposure, and wet and sometimes very cold winters. Looking also to the plants that naturally occur along the nearby coastline demonstrated that some ferns, as well as *Sedum* and *Achillea*, happily make their homes growing on or amongst the rocks.

Groups of mostly evergreen shrubs, such as *Salvia rosmarinus*, *Hebe*, *Santolina* or *Cotoneaster*, as well as the deciduous shrub *Potentilla fruticosa* and the grass *Sporobolus heterolepis*, are repeated throughout the front garden. These structural plants punctuate a matrix of the grass *Sesleria autumnalis* and herbaceous perennials that weave through the garden, offering both ground cover and seasonal highlights. Alpine plants seen primarily amongst rocks and along the edge of the path offer additional seasonal treats.

There is a succession of planting that provides food for wildlife and interest for people from early spring flowering, such as *Armeria maritima* and *A. juniperfolius*, *Pulsatilla vulgaris*, *Salvia rosmarinus*, and *Achillea × kellereri*.

Plants such as *Geranium* 'Dusky Crug' and *Persicaria affinis* have long flowering seasons, starting in late spring/early summer and continuing through the summer and into autumn. These were combined with *Sesleria autumnalis*, *Origanum* 'Herrenhausen', and *Hylotelephium* 'Matrona' to create a repeated informal pattern throughout the garden. At the height of the

Mounds of low planting and delicate grasses contrast with the carefully placed rocks in Rachel Bailey's naturalistic coastal garden (© Rachel Bailey).

Steps lead the visitor to the house through a tapestry of low planting amongst gravel and rocks (© Rachel Bailey).

summer are seasonal highlights of *Achillea* 'Anthea', *Campanula portenschlagiana*, *Limonium platyphyllum*, *Santolina pinnata* 'Edward Bowles', *Dianthus carthusianorum*, and *Sedum* 'Coral Carpet'.

As winter approaches, the garden continues to offer visual interest through seedheads, spent flower stems, structural shrubs, autumn colour of the foliage of *Persicaria* and *Sesleria*, and the movement from the grasses.

The garden importantly continues to provide habitats for wildlife. The berries of *Cotoneaster* will feed birds and mice, predators will feed on insect prey nestled in a spent flower head or flower stem, or amongst the foliage of the mat-forming plants such as *Acaena*, *Persicaria*, *Sedum* 'Coral Carpet', and *Campanula portenschlagiana* and the grassy hummocks of *Sesleria*.

The ground cover will also offer hiding places and allow movement through the garden for smaller organisms such as insects, whilst the repeated flowers will offer a large food source for pollinators over the summer and autumn months, in particular.

Connecting the garden to the stony and rocky coastline, the plants were planted into a deep gravel mulch to 'dress' the builders' rubble, suppress the seed bank in the 'soil' from germinating, and retain water in this exposed location. Open areas of gravel also offer open hunting ground for spiders and create spaces for ground-nesting insects, for example.

The rocks also provide shade and cool areas and nooks for both plants and wildlife that prefer some shelter and a cooler, damper environment. *Polypodium vulgare*, *Saxifraga × urbium* 'London Pride' and *Carex remota* were planted on the north aspect of the larger rocks. Frogs were also found overwintering within a pocket created between rocks.

Ed O'Brien Discusses his Recycled Rubble Garden in Bristol

This site, located in North Bristol, is a southeast facing front garden on a suburban road. The owner had a substantial amount of building waste left over from building works, which was recycled to create a low-nutrient planting substrate. It was a mixture of half sharp sand, half broken concrete, crushed brick, old plaster and other hardcore, laid to a depth of 30cm over a clay/loam subsoil.

The garden was planted in the autumn, following Peter Korn's (2018) method of planting perennials bareroot and washing any compost off the plants' roots, which is supposed to help them establish and send out deep roots. *Sesleria autumnalis* was used as the matrix grass, as it is evergreen and tends not to flop like stipas. *Hebe rakaiensis* and *Euphorbia characias* were also planted for structure. Around these plants, others were arranged at random in a matrix at a density of eight to ten plants per square metre. Successional bulbs were also planted at this time, and the garden was given an initial long soaking.

In late spring *Allium* 'Purple Sensation' is dotted through the textural planting in Ed O'Brien's front garden (© Ed O'Brien).

Later in the season yellow *Achillea* and purple *Nepeta* contrast with the silvery-white *Lychnis* (© Ed O'Brien).

The following spring, annuals such as cornflowers and Californian poppies were direct sown over the planting to fill any gaps present in the first year. The planting provided a long season of interest with crocuses, narcissi, tulips and alliums coming in waves until the perennials. Initially, the planting was mostly salvias, catmint and achilleas, but it was lacking in colour in late July and August, so eryngiums and echinaceas were added to keep the flowering going until the asters began.

Overall, the garden has been a great success. It has not needed watering in three years, despite several long droughts. Moreover, weeding has been minimal, perhaps an hour in the autumn, and the only other maintenance is the cutback at the start of February. This garden could be seen as a prototype for those seeking a naturalistic, low-maintenance front garden.

Table 17 Plants for Ed O'Brien's rubble garden

Perennials	Grasses
Hebe rakaiensis	Sesleria autumnalis
Euphorbia characias 'Humpty Dumpty'	Stipa gigantea
Calamintha nepeta 'Walker's Low'	
Salvia nemorosa 'Caradonna'	**Bulbs**
Achillea 'Terracotta', A. 'Moonshine'	Crocus (various species)
Euphorbia polychroma	Narcissus 'Ice Follies'
Lychnis coronaria 'Alba', L. 'Gardeners World'	Tulipa 'Dordogne'
Aster amellus 'Violet Queen'	Allium 'Purple Sensation'
Salvia × jamensis 'Nachtvlinder'	Allium 'Globemaster'
Pulsatilla vulgaris	
Eryngium planum 'Blue Glitter'	
Echinacea pallida, E. tennesseensis	

Management Considerations

There are various management considerations that are specifically relevant to the types of planting schemes discussed above. I have mentioned that with the right choice of plants, there is little need for irrigation or watering and, by reducing fertility, not only is there less competition, but there is also less need to stake species that are growing too tall and floppy. However, it is important to remember that the underlying soil will always affect the planting over the long-term and it is worth noting that research has shown that if substrates with fines are used, weed germination is more of a problem (Hitchmough and Livingstone, 2020).

In many of these schemes, perennials and grasses that have stood through the winter are cut back in February or March before any new growth appears and all the cuttings must be removed. Similarly, any dying plants that start decaying on the gravel should be removed. This is to ensure there is reduced fertility and to prevent a new organic layer developing on top of the mulch. Hollow stems that are cut back could be retained in places for wildlife but should be contained in bundles and perhaps raised off the ground.

There can also be an issue with deep-rooted weeds if they do manage to take a hold in the deep substrate. Once their roots penetrate the soil below, they will

Dead seed and flower heads are tied to a post in the Grasslands Garden to provide shelter for invertebrates.

become competitive and pulling up these weeds results in soil being brought to the surface, increasing fertility and bringing some of the buried seed bank to the light where they can germinate (Bower, 2021). Ensuring any tiny weeds are removed quickly can alleviate this problem. When I met with John Little, he told me that he weeds out undesirable self-seeded species before they get too big. He also explained that this is why he does not include grasses in his seed mixes. Grass seedlings are very difficult to differentiate, making early weeding almost impossible.

Finally, there is the issue of ecological succession. As I discussed in Chapter 1, secondary succession starts with the establishment of pioneer species and over decades the landscape eventually becomes a woodland. This is true on brownfield sites, although, because of contamination and harsh conditions, it may take time. Any dead or dying matter left on the mineral mulches in the gardens discussed in this chapter will gradually start to build up a new soil layer that eventually will develop to support new species. This means that management must be informed and knowledgeable as well as happening little and often, allowing for tweaks here and there. It may be that this sort of planting is not so suitable for small gardens where there are also trees, hedges and shrubs for seasonal interest and shelter for wildlife. In these spaces leaf fall could be a fairly constant problem.

Mediterranean Landscapes and Summer Dormancy

In Chapter 5 I discussed the difference in growing seasons between the UK and the Mediterranean. As the climate crisis proceeds, designers in the UK may need to learn from their counterparts in countries to the south in order to understand how to design for a summer dormant season rather than a winter one.

A Regenerated Coastal Landscape – Martí Franch

On the Cap de Creus Peninsula in northeast Catalonia, there is an unusual example of a regenerated Mediterranean landscape. This section of the National Park was formerly a Club Med tourist enclave, complete with low-rise stone cabins and paved access routes.

Phlomis growing wild on a rocky mountainside in Crete (© Sergio Denche).

Landscape architect, Martí Franch, worked with a team of collaborators and experts to restore the landscape while also introducing subtle contemporary elements that hint at the history of the site (Heatherington, 2021). Salvaged stone was reused, viewpoints created, and new paths still follow some of the existing routes. All the invasive vegetation was removed and recycled: in fact, over 95 per cent of the waste was recycled on site (Ybern, 2012).

Native species have been allowed to recolonise the landscape from the existing seed bank and observation of this successional process can serve as inspiration for designers working with rocky, exposed, coastal sites. All the vegetation is low-growing, sometimes forming tapestries of different species, and clinging to rocks or erupting in little crevices and in sheltered spots between boulders (Heatherington, 2021). There are mounds of *Crithmum maritimum*, sometimes known as rock samphire, with its succulent grey-green leaves and greenish-yellow flowers that, in the UK, last from late spring through the summer. Low-growing

stonecrop, *Sedum sediforme*, also forms low evergreen mounds and flowers in summer and *Juniperus oxycedrus*, in these conditions, is a stunted, low-growing evergreen conifer that hugs the bare rock in green mounds (Heatherington, 2021). Amongst the matrix of lower-growing vegetation is the umbellifer, *Daucus gingidium* (sea carrot), and *Lagurus ovatus*, an annual grass in the UK with long-lasting attractive, furry flowers like little bunny tails.

Left: Vegetation begins to recolonise the new interventions on the Cap de Creus Peninsula, designed by Martí Franch and Ardèvols Associates. Below: Sweeps of native vegetation, including *Lagurus ovatus* and *Crithmum maritimum*, regenerating in a low, slightly sheltered valley on the Cap de Creus Peninsula, designed by Martí Franch and Ardèvols Associates.

A Landscape in Greece – Thomas Doxiadis

Landscape architect, Thomas Doxiadis's, designs for an extensive landscape around a complex of new villas in Greece demonstrates how to integrate new gardens into a sensitive and endangered place (Doxiadis, n.d.). As he explains to Louisa Jones (2011: p.30), 'this is a landscape where windswept vegetation stays low. Everything you do shows up immediately'. He works with indigenous plants, allowing them to appear to disperse out from the inhabited space into the wider landscape beyond. The result is a pattern of interweaving shapes – cushions, mounds and balls – that play with shades of grey, yellow, orange and green. In spring there may briefly be flowers, but by the summer these are gone, and the design relies on the forms and muted colours of the foliage that echo the tones of the surrounding rock and the simple paths. Light and shadow create the rhythms in this design, rather than dramatic colours or contrasting forms.

To achieve this subtle, naturalistic effect, Doxiadis uses percentages of plants, changing the mix in different sections; this ensures there is continuity, whilst also creating slight changes to attract attention as you explore. Nearer the houses he plants at a higher density, and this is reduced as the gardens merge into the landscape. At a certain distance no new plants are added and a natural re-vegetation is allowed to take place (Doxiadis, n.d.). Species include the low mounds of *Centaurea spinosa*, *Limoniastrum monopetalum* and *Sarcopoterium spinosum* and the yellow-flowered *Calendula arvensis*, *Inula viscosa* and *Chrysanthemum coronarium*. To these are added a mix of native varieties of *Cistus*, *Thymus* and *Origanum* (Jones, 2011).

A path to the sea through a landscape of low mounded shrubs in Antiparos, Greece, designed by Thomas Doxiadis (© Clive Nichols).

A Dry, Rocky Mediterranean Garden – Olivier Filippi

Olivier Filippi embraces summer dormancy using the dry, rocky Mediterranean landscapes as inspiration for his planting designs. In his own garden he has experimented with mounded gravel beds, 60–80cm deep (Bruce, 2020), and drought-tolerant species that form hummocks in various shades of muted silvers, greys, greeny-blues and browns (Filippi, 2019). Sub-shrubs are chosen for their form, leaf colour, texture and aromatic qualities rather than their flowers and are interspersed with accents of cypress, *Cupressus sempervirens* Stricta Group, gnarled olive trees and the distinctive forms of pine trees, *Pinus pinea*.

Designer Olivier Filippi's gravel garden in Meze, France, in the dawn sunlight (© Clive Nichols).

Nevertheless, there are flowers in the garden: they include the white of *Cistus* × *cyprius* f. *albiflorus*, the pink-purple and yellow *Phlomis purpurea* 'Torcal de Antequera' and *Phlomis longifolia,* and the pink knapweed, *Centaurea bella* (Bruce, n.d.), that makes a silvery ground cover and flowers in spring. But by the end of May most of the flowers are over and it is the trees and low shrubs that give seasonal structure and introduce a rhythm into the design. The result is a textural tapestry of forms and subtle colours that attract the attention throughout the year.

Like Thomas Rainer (2018), who I discussed in Chapter 4, Filippi (2018) explains that it is those who manage the garden who decide on the aesthetic: this is where the creativity happens. In the deep gravel of his garden *Euphorbia rigida*, for example, 'self-seeds like crazy' (Filippi, 2018) and decisions must be taken about where to weed it out and when to keep it.

Using Allelopathic Plants

Allelopathic plants are those which produce chemicals that have an effect (that could be positive or negative) on other plants, influencing germination, development and survival. Filippi (2018) utilises this property in his garden to reduce competition and suppress weed growth. He gives an example of the decomposing felt-like leaves of *Phlomis* that fall to the ground next to the plant early in the summer and then emit chemicals that inhibit germination in other species (Basson, 2019). Other allelopathic plants that Filippi uses in his gardens include *Rosmarinus officinalis*, *Santolina magonica*, and *Helichrysum italicum* (Filippi, 2018).

Using plants in this way has potential, but I suspect it is more complicated than it appears. The black walnut is probably the best-known example of an allelopathic tree but, even in this instance, research appears to give conflicting results (Chalker-Scott, 2019). And personally, I have found that weeds have no problem growing beneath rosemary bushes.

CHAPTER 7

DESIGNING FOR WILDLIFE

Gardens in Britain cover a huge area – the RHS (2021c) estimates it is nearly 730,000 hectares – and thus they are a wonderful resource with the potential to create habitats for wildlife in both urban and rural areas. When designing for the climate crisis and creating sustainable gardens, we should always consider how best to cater for wildlife as well as human inhabitants. And this applies to the whole of the garden rather than just leaving a small overgrown section as a 'wildlife habitat'.

Creating spaces for nature in a garden is not as simple as just leaving it to go 'wild'; this results in decreased rather than increased diversity when competitive species such as brambles take over. The term rewilding is not always a useful one when thinking about creating and managing our gardens. The designer and presenter Joe Swift comments:

'People ask me, how can I rewild my 50ft garden in Hackney? And the answer is, you can't. You can make it wilder, more naturalistic, more biodiverse and all those things that gardeners do to manipulate the space they've got, but to recreate nature completely in a garden is impossible really.' (Heath, 2022).

Isabella Tree at Knepp (*see* below) outlines what designing for wildlife really means in practice: 'There's a common misconception that it's about doing nothing, "letting nature take over". But turning your back on a garden... is not the way to improve it for wildlife' (Tree, 2023).

If we leave a garden to its own devices, it will fairly quickly become a mass of brambles and bindweed – it will be less diverse rather than the opposite. Eventually, as I discussed in Chapter 1, trees will colonise the space and reduced light levels will result in fewer lower-growing species and in turn this means there will be fewer invertebrates and other wildlife. As Tree (2023) explains 'a garden is only complex and species-rich because of the interventions of the gardener'.

In fact, we need to embrace and nurture a relationship between humans and nature, working together to create sustainable and environmentally friendly gardens. And this can happen in a surprising multitude of ways. As Alex Johnson and I show in our book, *Habitat Creation in Garden Design* (2022), it does not mean that gardens need to be messy, weedy patches of scrubby vegetation, nor do we have to just plant native species. In fact, wildlife gardens can be exciting, creative and innovative contemporary spaces that make links with the architecture that surrounds them, enthral the people who visit them and support a diverse range of plants, birds, mammals and invertebrates. Many of the key interventions we make to attract these creatures also help us to design these gardens to be a delight throughout the year.

Elephant hawk moth on unmown grass in an urban front garden (© Oli Holmes).

One of the first things to consider is whether any of the trees and shrubs or other habitats in the garden can be retained. This is a sustainable approach that should be the starting point of any design. Wildlife habitats take years to establish and therefore if there are any on site that are thriving, perhaps they should form a part of the new garden (Gaston *et al.*, 2005). However, in small gardens especially, plants need to earn their keep: it is preferable that a tree or shrub has more than one season of interest, providing blossom and berries for example, and therefore it may be desirable to make changes.

Food, Shelter and Water

In order to attract wild creatures and provide a safe and productive environment in which they can not only survive, but also breed, we need to consider three elements: food, shelter and water. In the following sections I outline the successional impact of considering these three factors when designing a garden.

Food

Nectar, pollen, leaves, fruit, berries, seeds, nuts and decaying matter are all valuable foods for the wildlife in our gardens. Many insects including bees, hoverflies, butterflies and moths feed on nectar, and pollen is collected by pollinators to feed their young. This is a necessary stage in the fertilisation of plants, the formation of fruits and seeds and hence the creation of a new generation and it is therefore also a crucial part of our food production process.

Caterpillars feed on leaves and they, in turn, are food for baby birds such as blue and great tits, and fruit and berries are an invaluable food source for birds in the autumn and winter months – many migrating birds stop in our gardens to feast on berries. Birds and small

A gatekeeper butterfly on wild carrot – note the distinctive curling up of the seedhead.

A female blackcap about to enjoy the berries of an *Amelanchier*.

mammals enjoy seeds and nuts through the winter, sometimes caching them for use in the colder periods, and fallen apples and pears are also a good food source.

Finally, there are rotting leaves and other vegetation that are drawn down into the soil by earthworms, and fallen logs and branches are a source of food for beetles and other detritivores.

Table 18 Wildlife and seasonal succession – food

Wildlife Considerations	Examples beneficial for wildlife and for seasonal succession (*see also* Heatherington and Johnson, 2022)
Nectar and Pollen Pollinators come in all shapes and sizes, and this determines the species of flower they feed on. It is the tongue length of the pollinator that determines whether they can access nectar from a flower, therefore different shapes and forms of flower heads attract different species of pollinator. When planting for pollinators and for succession we need to choose a diverse range of species and also to select plants that flower both early and late in the season to ensure there is plenty of food for as long as possible. Long-flowering varieties are also useful.	• *Erysimum* 'Bowles's Mauve' is sterile but provides nectar and is long flowering. • *Abelia* × *grandiflora* is a semi-evergreen with late, sweet-scented flowers. • *Crataegus laevigata* 'Crimson Cloud' is a cultivar of the native hawthorn with bright pink flowers and purple/red haws. • The native selfheal, *Prunella vulgaris*, is a source of nectar throughout the summer and can establish in flowering lawns and even as a ground cover under taller plants.
Leaves We may not want caterpillars to eat the leaves of our favourite plants, but it is surprising how many there are in the garden doing just that without us noticing. In order to attract birds into the garden, we need to provide food for their babies as well as for the adults. It is not necessary to know exactly which leaf is eaten by which caterpillar, unless we are trying to attract a particular species that is present in the local area, but we can provide a range of shrubs to provide food and interest through much of the year.	• Fruit trees are a useful food source and can be trained as fans and espaliers in a more formal scheme. • The mullein caterpillar feeds on native *Verbascum* but also likes closely related cultivars. Verbascums are dramatic accent plants and useful in a design as they keep their seedheads through the winter. • The caterpillar of the holly blue feeds on the native evergreens – holly and ivy.
Fruit and berries Fruit and berries are as attractive in the autumn and winter to the human visitor as they are to the wildlife. Vibrant red and orange berries stand out in the low autumn sunlight and apples and pears look beautiful ripening on the tree before being picked. Some of the windfalls can be left on the ground for the wildlife to enjoy.	• *Ilex aquifolium* is a native evergreen shrub/tree with red berries. It can be used in a mixed hedge. • *Pyracantha* ssp. are evergreen with spring flowers and wonderful crops of orange, red or gold berries. • The native *Sorbus aucuparia* has clusters of bright orange berries.
Seeds and nuts Nuts do not last long on trees if there are squirrels and mice around, but the seedheads of flowers and grasses stand into the winter months creating stark sculptural forms and glowing in the low sunlight.	• The native *Corylus avellana* can be coppiced to create a multi-stemmed tree with catkins in winter and nuts later in the summer. • Members of the thistle family as well as teasel have long-lasting seedheads that attract goldfinches especially. • Sunflowers provide nectar, and then seeds and shelter, as well as having a dramatic winter presence.

Shelter

The masses in the garden, especially the trees, shrubs and hedges provide dense shelter for all sorts of wildlife to roost in, hibernate, hide from predators, rear their young and as a vantage point when searching for food. Evergreens provide important shelter, especially in the winter, and low vegetation is a place for invertebrates to hide. Crevices in bark and holes in tree trunks are also useful habitats and skeleton stems provide places for small invertebrates to overwinter.

The pitted trunk of an ancient olive provides many cracks and crevices in which wildlife can shelter (© Sergio Denche).

Table 19 Wildlife and seasonal succession – shelter

Wildlife Considerations	Examples beneficial for wildlife and for seasonal succession, (*see also* Heatherington and Johnson, 2022)
Trees, shrubs and hedges Choosing a range of trees, shrubs and incorporating a hedge into the design of the warp can help to keep interest in the garden throughout the year and is also beneficial for wildlife. Selecting trees and shrubs with peeling, cracked or gnarled bark provides winter interest for us and crevices for the creatures to hide in.	• *Acer campestre* 'William Caldwell' is a cultivar of the native species, attractive to pollinators and has orange and red autumn colour. • *Hippophae rhamnoides* is a native shrub with silvery leaves and bright orange berries. • The native tree *Carpinus betulus* makes an interesting hedge, keeping its dead leaves through the winter.
Evergreens Evergreens can be used for winter interest and as framing and punctuation plants. Some of their flowers, such as *Mahonia*, have a lovely scent to attract late-flying bees. *Mahonia* also produces early berries in April and May.	• *Taxus baccata*, the native yew, makes dense cover and can be clipped to create interesting forms. • *Taxus baccata* 'Fastigiata' is a good anchoring and accent plant. • Native *Luzula sylvatica* is semi-evergreen and good for ground cover in damp shade.
Flowering lawns and ground cover Allowing a lawn to grow longer and to support wildflower species adds interest and colour to what would normally be a uniform green void. As with all planting choices, it is best to select a diverse range of ground cover species for interest throughout the year and to create a range of habitats. This can be determined by the frequency of mowing.	• Dandelion, clover, buttercup, daisy and selfheal are among the many species that will thrive in a lawn if it is not mown for some months of the summer.
Dead flower and grass stems The way a flower or grass dies and whether it survives into the winter months can determine whether your planting scheme has autumn and winter drama and interest.	• *Dipsacus fullonum*, native teasel, keeps its seedheads for months, often into the following year. • *Cynara cardunculus* is loved by bumble bees for its nectar and pollen and keeps its distinctive dead seedheads through the winter. Silvery-grey leaves emerge in late winter.

An interlacing matrix of perennials and grasses with layers of shrubs and trees provides an abundance of food and shelter for wildlife (© Alex Johnson).

Water

A pond is a delight at any time of the year; reflections bring dynamism to the garden and play with the different light levels in the changing seasons. Even a small area of still water, designed for wildlife, attracts birds and mammals to feed, drink and wash but if there is not space for a pond, including a basin or bowl is also beneficial, providing a welcome drink for birds. Moving water adds sound to the plays of light, creating a distinctive atmosphere, and provides a different habitat from a still pool, attracting larger species to drink and bathe.

Amphibians breed in ponds and many invertebrates spend all or part of their life cycle in water and therefore the planted edges of ponds are important as they provide shelter and a vantage point for creatures as they enter or leave the pond. Some invertebrates lay their eggs on overhanging plants or use them during the transition from the larval to the adult stage.

Top left: A sculptural water bowl designed by Sarah Walton creates a focal point framed by a yew hedge and surrounded by alliums, iris and *Phlomis*. Top right: A broad bodied chaser on the edge of a pond in a contemporary London garden designed for wildlife.

Table 20 Wildlife and seasonal succession – water

Wildlife Considerations	Examples beneficial for wildlife and for seasonal succession, (*see also* Heatherington and Johnson, 2022)
Ponds and pools Marginal plants and floating aquatics often have unusual textural leaves that add interest. However, these do die back in the winter, therefore, siting rocks where they can be seen from the house on a winter's day is a good way to keep the attention – sometimes there will be a bird to watch as it has a quick drink perched on the rocks and pebbles.	• Non-native plants can be invasive in water and therefore it is best to use native plants when designing a pond. Examples include *Stratiotes aloides*, *Myriophyllum spicatum* and *Myosotis scorpioides*. • *Hottonia palustris*, the native water violet, has whorled feathery leaves that last into the autumn and pale, purple flowers in late spring.
Moving water As with the pond, marginal planting can be chosen to add to the drama and bulbs included to give interest early in the season.	• Candelabra primulas like boggy conditions and look good when sited beside a moving stream, but these are not native. The native cowslip *Primula veris* makes a good alternative and is attractive to wildlife. • Grasses with a fountain-like form look good beside water. If the soil is not damp, try *Pennisetum alopecuroides* 'Hameln' or *P.* 'Black Beauty'. Both have wonderful caterpillar-like flowers in summer.

Table 20 (*Cont'd*)

Wildlife Considerations	Examples beneficial for wildlife and for seasonal succession, (*see also* Heatherington and Johnson, 2022)
Pond edges Edges can be designed with layers of textural planting that concentrate on leaf form with a few splashes of colour, usually early in the year.	• Native *Filipendula ulmaria* is food for moth larvae with a mass of cream flowers that look good at the water's edge. Combines well with the cultivar of another native, *Lythrum salicaria* 'Blush'. • *Helleborus foetidus* is a native evergreen with pale green flowers in winter that associates well with water. Combine with hostas for contrasting textures. • In dappled shade, plant evergreen ferns such as the giant *Woodwardia fimbriata*.

Early flowers of *Darmera peltata* push through the dense foliage of *Leucojum* that provides shelter on the edge of a pond in Beth Chatto's Garden.

Designing for Wildlife using Mineral Mulches

Knepp Castle Estate in the south of England is known for its innovative rewilding project in which the family estate, which was originally intensively farmed, is now being allowed to develop, as much as is feasible for a relatively small site, through natural processes (Tree, 2018). Free-roaming grazing animals – old breeds of domesticated cattle, pigs and ponies, as well as deer – mimic the behaviour of herbivores that would have originally grazed the land and this helps to drive what is described as a 'process-led regeneration' (Rewilding Britain, 2023). This is work in progress and it will be interesting to see how it develops over the years.

Recently, the Estate has created a garden for wildlife that extrapolates some of the principles behind the rewilding of landscapes to introduce a diversity of habitats, thus supporting a wide range of invertebrates and birds. The ground plane of the site has been excavated to create hollows and mounds, similar to John Little's garden in the previous chapter, but with more extreme changes in level. The substrate is a mix of crushed brick and concrete at different depths, and designers, Tom Stuart-Smith and James Hitchmough, have created planting palettes that include 900 species (Tree, 2023). Many are perennials and grasses from the Mediterranean and the Southern Hemisphere and there are also trees and shrubs to provide layers of shelter.

The result is a garden in which beautiful dynamic waves of different colours and textures come and go through the seasons, providing interest for people and habitats for wildlife. Underpinning the decision-making process and the design of this garden is a willingness on the part of the 'rewilding gardener' (Tree, 2023) to take an experimental approach that attempts to learn lessons from how nature behaves, and to apply and refine them over time in the management of this garden.

Left: View across the walled garden on the Knepp Castle Estate, designed by Tom Stuart-Smith and James Hitchmough. Below: One of the many micro habitats to be found at Knepp.

Layers

For gardens to fulfil their potential as wildlife habitats they need to extend out into the wider landscape, joining up with other gardens and green spaces to make continuous wildlife corridors. These connections between layers of vegetation over large areas ensure creatures can move between spaces and have many opportunities to search for food, defend territories, find mates and much more. It is easy for the gardener to leave gaps along the boundaries to facilitate this freedom of movement. When deciding on the plant palette, it is always useful to observe what is growing happily in neighbouring gardens and even to think about how views can be enhanced by the trees and shrubs that are thriving over the fence.

Creatures in search of food and shelter move through the horizontal and vertical layers that make up a garden – the masses in a design. In contrast, people tend to occupy the voids. Good design for wildlife, and for seasonal succession, has a high level of spatial complexity; layers of vegetation ensure that there is a diversity of habitats for a range of creatures as well as helping to frame the spaces in the garden and provide varied experiences through the changing seasons (Heatherington and Johnson, 2022). As I discussed in Chapter 2, the imperative to design with the climate crisis in mind also informs our choice of plant combinations and suggests that we should be planting a range of species to ensure the survival of some during uncertain conditions (Heatherington, 2021). Interestingly, it has been shown that, as well as

This front garden, designed by the author, includes layers of trees and shrubs, winding frames of box and a mass of rippling perennials and grasses.

being beneficial for wildlife, complex landscapes tend to contribute to human well-being (Cameron *et al.*, 2020).

I have mentioned how some designers use the concept of layers when creating their planting schemes: examples include Thomas Rainer's ecological horticulture and the forest gardens in Chapter 4. Alex Johnson and I (2022) draw on an ecological system of layers that includes the canopy, understorey, field and ground layers, when discussing designing habitats for wildlife in gardens. The ground and field layers can be thought of as the layer of low-growing shrubs and ground cover; the understorey can be divided into several sub-layers, a shrub and tall herbaceous layer, hedges and larger shrubs, and a transitional layer that includes climbers and multi-stemmed trees. Thinking about designing in three dimensions and focusing on how these layers interrelate is part of the challenge of creating a spatially complex garden that embraces the horizontal and the vertical planes through the lens of time.

A Family Garden for Wildlife

This urban garden was designed for a client who loved plants and wanted to attract wildlife, while also ensuring there were secret spaces for her children to play and run around in. The garden needed to link with the contemporary new extension to the house and provide

Textural layers of planting in this small shady town garden provide shelter and interest throughout the year. Design by the author.

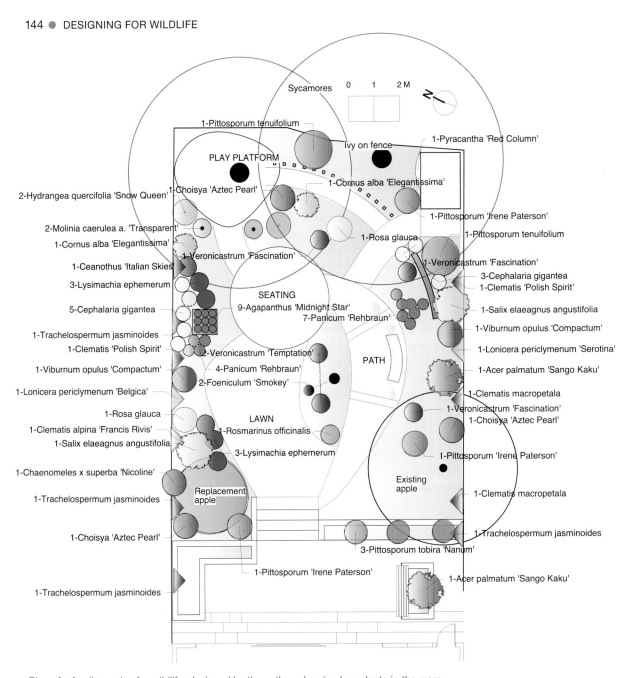

Sycamores

0   1   2 M

1-Pittosporum tenuifolium

1-Pyracantha 'Red Column'

PLAY PLATFORM

Ivy on fence

1-Cornus alba 'Elegantissima'

2-Hydrangea quercifolia 'Snow Queen'

1-Choisya 'Aztec Pearl'

1-Pittosporum 'Irene Paterson'

2-Molinia caerulea a. 'Transparent'

1-Pittosporum tenuifolium

1-Cornus alba 'Elegantissima'

1-Rosa glauca

1-Ceanothus 'Italian Skies'

1-Veronicastrum 'Fascination'

1-Veronicastrum 'Fascination'

3-Lysimachia ephemerum

3-Cephalaria gigantea

1-Clematis 'Polish Spirit'

5-Cephalaria gigantea

SEATING

1-Salix elaeagnus angustifolia

9-Agapanthus 'Midnight Star'

1-Trachelospermum jasminoides

7-Panicum 'Rehbraun'

1-Viburnum opulus 'Compactum'

1-Clematis 'Polish Spirit'

1-Lonicera periclymenum 'Serotina'

1-Viburnum opulus 'Compactum'

2-Veronicastrum 'Temptation'

PATH

1-Acer palmatum 'Sango Kaku'

4-Panicum 'Rehbraun'

1-Lonicera periclymenum 'Belgica'

2-Foeniculum 'Smokey'

1-Clematis macropetala

1-Veronicastrum 'Fascination'

1-Rosa glauca

1-Choisya 'Aztec Pearl'

LAWN

1-Clematis alpina 'Francis Rivis'

1-Rosmarinus officinalis

1-Salix elaeagnus angustifolia

1-Pittosporum 'Irene Paterson'

3-Lysimachia ephemerum

1-Chaenomeles x superba 'Nicoline'

Existing
apple

1-Trachelospermum jasminoides

1-Clematis macropetala

Replacement
apple

1-Choisya 'Aztec Pearl'

1-Trachelospermum jasminoides

3-Pittosporum tobira 'Nanum'

1-Pittosporum 'Irene Paterson'

1-Acer palmatum 'Sango Kaku'

1-Trachelospermum jasminoides

Plan of a family garden for wildlife, designed by the author, showing key plants in the warp.

areas to relax and entertain. It benefitted from two mature sycamores at the rear and two wonderful apple trees near the house. Unfortunately, one of the apples was found to be rotten and had to be removed, but some of the wood was used to make the children's play platform round the sycamore. The design weaves paths through the colourful planting, in and out of the roofed platform and past log stepping posts, as well as giving access to the shed and the circular seating area in the sun. The lawn is kept small to allow space for the large beds with their vertical layers.

The mature trees provide a ready-made canopy layer that is enhanced by the addition of smaller species such as *Acer* 'Sango Kaku'. *Pittosporum* ssp., *Hydrangea quercifolia*, *Choisya* 'Aztec Pearl' and *Salix elaeagnus angustifolia* are included in the shrub

Digitalis ferruginea in front of Corten screen with *Veronicastrum virginicum* 'Fascination', *Veronica spicata incana* 'Nana' and *Hakonechloa macra* in the foreground. The path leads to the play platform.

Digitalis ferruginea is interlaced with *Panicum* 'Rehbraun', *Macleaya microcarpa* 'Spetchley Ruby' and dots of *Crocosmia* 'Lucifer'.

Lysimachia ephemerum and *Digitalis ferruginea* are dotted through clusters of *Achillea* 'Summer Wine' and *Aster pyrenaeus* 'Lutetia' in this view back towards the house and the raised patio.

layer. The tall herbaceous layer contains perennials such as *Veronicastrum virginicum* 'Fascination', *Cephalaria gigantea*, *Lysimachia ephemerum*, *Foeniculum vulgare* 'Smoky' and the grasses, *Molinia* 'Transparent' and *Panicum* 'Rehbraun' all of which have an autumn and sometimes a winter presence. Climbers, including early- and late-flowering honeysuckles, *Lonicera* 'Belgica' and *L.* 'Serotina', create the transition layer and cover the boundary fences, giving interest and cover for much of the year. The scent of honeysuckle is strongest at night when it can attract moths, and the berries are a food source for birds. Clematis in the transition layer have a fine display of flowers and not only provide shelter, but are also a food source for caterpillars (Butterfly conservation, n.d.). Retaining walls and raised beds next to the patio raise plants up to inhabit the middle layers of the garden, as does the large Corten planter containing *Agapanthus*, which forms a focal point near the circular seating area. The inclusion of some evergreen shrubs ensures cover for the wildlife through the winter and the different leaf textures add interest.

In the low shrub layer are *Lavandula* and several domed evergreen *Hebe* ssp., both attractive to pollinators, and *Buxus* to provide shelter, as well as the distinctive form of *Cotoneaster horizontalis* with its berries that often last until late winter. Perennials and grasses are mainly planted in clusters; it is interesting to note that pollinators tend to conserve energy by feeding on larger patches of the same flower (Heatherington and Johnson, 2022). The list below gives a selection of some of the grasses, perennials and ferns used in this garden, many chosen for their attractiveness to wildlife and their long-lasting presence.

Table 21 Plant list for the family wildlife garden

Perennials, grasses and ferns	Bulbs and fillers
Achillea 'Summer Wine'	Anthriscus sylvestris
Amsonia tabernaemontana	'Ravenswing'
Artemisia dracunculus	Digitalis ferruginea
Aster pyrenaeus 'Lutetia'	Verbena bonariensis
Cirsium rivulare	Allium 'Purple Sensation'
'Atropurpureum'	Allium schoenoprasum
Geranium macrorrhizum	'Forescate'
'White Ness'	Nectaroscordum siculum
Heuchera 'Rachel'	Narcissus poeticus recurvus
Origanum vulgare	
'Thumble's Variety'	
Salvia officinalis	
purpurascens	
Hylotelephium 'Bertram	
Anderson'	
Tiarella cordifolia	
Veronica spicata incana	
'Nana'	
Calamagrostis brachytricha	
Hakonechloa macra	
Athyrium niponicum var.	
pictum	
Polypodium interjectum	
'Cornubiense'	
Polystichum setiferum	
'Herrenhausen'	

Aster pyrenaeus 'Lutetia', *Veronica spicata incana* 'Nana' and *Hakonechloa macra* tumble over the wide, curved path.

These perennials and grasses wind through the taller species and even find their way into pockets in the wide, curving path. The resulting planting flows through both horizontal and vertical planes, connecting the different layers, providing food through the seasons, and cover and safe ways for creatures to travel. The dense planting and wide range of flowers, berries and leaf textures create interest, and the design of the paths and seating areas allows the human inhabitants to get up close and to fully immerse themselves in the garden.

Natives and Non-Natives

There is an assumption that when designing for wildlife we should only use native plants. However, in domestic gardens this is not necessarily the case. There are some creatures that are specialists, requiring a particular species for their survival, but many of the birds and invertebrates coming to our gardens are generalists – they can feed on a variety of foods and thrive in a range of habitats.

Research by the RHS (2021a) has shown that, although native plants provide the best habitats for invertebrates, plants from the northern hemisphere are almost as good and even those from the southern hemisphere have a part to play. The latter can provide much-needed evergreen winter cover (Salisbury *et al.*, 2017). Similarly, the numbers of pollinators,

such as bumblebees, solitary bees and hoverflies, visiting native and northern hemisphere species was slightly higher than those coming to southern hemisphere plants, but these could be used to add to the diversity and extend the flowering season (Salisbury *et al.*, 2015) (Rollings and Goulson, 2019).

There is a plethora of information about which plants are best for pollinators, some of it perhaps not based on detailed research. The best place to start is the RHS *Plants for Pollinators* lists (RHS, 2021b), which are available online. They also have a little bee symbol beside each plant on their website to indicate whether it is a pollinator-friendly species. There are several other clues as to whether a particular flower might be suitable:

- Does it have single or double flowers? Single flowering species are more likely to be attractive to pollinators because the nectar is more accessible. Double flowers may not have any nectar or what there is may be inaccessible.
- Is it repeat or long-flowering? These varieties are beneficial to wildlife and great for a successional garden. *Geranium* 'Rozanne' flowers throughout the summer and is very attractive to solitary bees (Rollings, 2019). However, some highly bred plant species may not be fertile and may therefore not have any nectar.
- Is it scented? This may indicate that it is attractive to pollinators. Night-scented species often attract moths.
- What is the shape of the flower (*see* Chapter 2)? This gives an indication of the type of insect that can access the nectar. Bees and butterflies with longer tongues can reach down into tube-like flower heads, and umbellifers, with their flat, open heads consisting of clusters of tiny flowers, are attractive to hoverflies with shorter tongues.
- Is it a cultivar of a native species? More research is needed in this area, but it may be that cultivars retain some of the native's attractive qualities (Goulson, 2020).

Ultimately, choosing a diverse range of plants that flower over an extended period and, if possible, also including some native species, helps to ensure that the garden is attractive to wildlife and people alike.

Clusters of planting provide a long season of nectar and pollen at the RSPB garden, designed by the author with Alex Johnson. A native hedge forms a boundary and provides shelter and food (© Alex Johnson).

Fruit and Nut Trees

Planting fruit trees is a way of introducing layers for wildlife, while also ensuring there is year-round interest for humans: in winter their sculptural forms speak of age and weathering; spring brings blossom, often scent and the buzzing of bees and other pollinating insects; in summer, grasses and wildflowers grow in dappled shade and the fruit starts to form; finally from midsummer into autumn, there are crops of plums, gages, apples, pears, quinces and more – the yellows, purples, golds and reds are a feast for the eye as well as the palate. One unusual choice of fruit tree for a small garden is the medlar: it is an easy tree to grow and is great for pollinators.

If you are lucky enough to have space for an orchard, a grid of trees with mown paths running through them creates a pleasing order to the design; the trees are anchoring plants, around which flow the dots of colour and waves of green of an interlacing meadow. There are so many fruit trees to choose from that you can have blossom for several months in spring. If you have space for only one or two, they can also be trained along a wall or other support (*see* Chapter 8) and in this

A community orchard at Broomfield Park in London.

case, they become a frame for the lower planting at their feet. Or in a small garden a single tree can be planted in a flowering lawn with a chair beneath its spreading branches in the dappled shade.

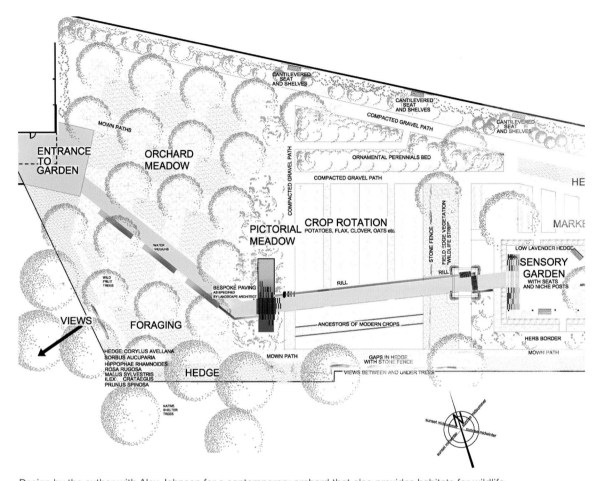

Design by the author with Alex Johnson for a contemporary orchard that also provides habitats for wildlife.

The Benefits of Unmown Grass

Research (Plantlife, n.d.-a) shows that if you allow areas of shorter and longer grass in a garden, diversity of plant species increases and wildlife will benefit. Plantlife suggest cutting the shorter sections every four weeks and leaving longer grass through the summer. In the mown areas bird's foot trefoil, white clover and selfheal thrive, and in the unmown grass ox-eye daisy, knapweed, field scabious and red clover will start to establish. In this way, you can design a path or small seating area in the lawn and be surrounded by the humming of insects at your feet and the delights of the fruits above you. The flowering period is extended through the summer, and you can also make the most of your unmown areas by planting a plethora of spring bulbs. Letting the grass grow and seeing what species appear and then allowing them to set seed before mowing brings an element of chance into the design of the weft, but it is also possible to remove sections of turf and seed, or plant plugs of native species into the lawn before sitting back and seeing which will happily dot themselves around.

Layers of Underplanting

Multi-stemmed and coppiced trees can bring structure and form to a design and also the opportunity to create expanses of ever-changing ground cover planting beneath their branches. The trees are the anchoring plants, and the perennials interlace and self-seed through the weft below, creating layers of shelter and with the potential to provide food for wildlife. It is important not to exclude light altogether, but to get the right balance between sun and shade. Always consider the mature size of the tree when placing it in the design.

The Nuttery at Sissinghurst is a wonderful example of this approach. Rows of coppiced hazels are underplanted with a tapestry of woodland species (Champion, 2014). Champion discusses how in early spring there are anemones, primroses, cowslips and violets. Then come acid yellows, lime greens and whites – *Smyrnium perfoliatum, Veratrum* ssp., *Euphorbia amygdaloides* var. *robbiae* – and ferns, *Matteuccia struthiopteris* and *Onoclea sensibilis*. Later, there are the deep blues and pinky-purples of *Omphalodes cappadocica* 'Cherry Ingram', *Lilium martagon* and *Dactylorhiza* × *grandis* (Champion, 2014).

An interlacing planting scheme can easily be designed for a smaller space than Sissinghurst and would work under a single fruit tree or a coppiced hazel. There are many choices of species for underplanting, and the selection is dependent on the particular growing conditions. Taking inspiration from what is around you and from how plant communities behave in nature is a good starting point. The designer Dan Pearson (2018) describes seeing *Lilium martagon* and *Astrantia* growing under nut trees on a mountainside in Northern Spain, and this combination with the addition of ripples of an evergreen ground cover such as *Epimedium* or clusters of hellebores or geraniums could easily be incorporated into a seasonal planting scheme for a small garden.

Death and Decay

Although I have asserted that wildlife gardens do not need to be messy, it is important to allow an element of untidiness, leaving fallen leaves and rotting wood or letting grass grow longer and vegetation intermingle at the base of a hedge. This expands the number of habitats the garden can support and therefore creates more opportunities for creatures to thrive. There is still a place for a more managed approach, but in embracing death and decay we can encourage wildlife and also find ways to enjoy the dormant season. The browns of bare earth, fallen leaves and dying flowers are often not visually appealing and many gardeners get pleasure from cutting back and tidying their gardens in the autumn, leaving little or no cover for overwintering invertebrates and birds, and also leaving little interest for people venturing outside in the winter months. Perhaps we need to find beauty in the browns. A dying flower can indeed be beautiful in its own way, but it is harder when faced with the dead leaves, stems and flowers flopped in a mass over the soil. Choosing species with long-lasting seedheads and a strong skeleton structure is one answer. Another is to enliven the scene with bright red and orange berries, silver bark and bare coloured stems in purples, fiery oranges and deep reds.

Ultimately, the balance between decay and order is in the hands of the people who will be enjoying and managing the garden. It may be necessary to compromise in some areas, but not in others and decisions can change over time.

Dead seedheads and stems are suspended from telegraph posts to continue providing shelter in John Little's garden in Essex.

CHAPTER 8

MANAGEMENT

In this chapter we will explore some of the key management issues to think about when designing for succession. You will discover the difference between intensive and extensive maintenance, as well as reiterating the importance of retaining dead seedheads and flower stems and the implications of allowing plants to self-seed. I include two tables, one outlining some of the general maintenance tasks to be undertaken throughout the year, and the second looking at the more detailed maintenance requirements of the college garden that I discussed in Chapter 3.

General Monthly Maintenance

Although much of the general management in any garden can be applied to the successional garden, there are some areas that need to be emphasised or adapted. As I have discussed in Chapter 5, an understanding of the pruning requirements of each plant is crucial to ensure flowers, berries and stem colour are allowed to develop to their best advantage. It is also important to leave the dead and dying flowers, stems and seeds for as long as possible to give structure and to provide

Seedheads and dead flower heads are lit by the low sun at Scampston in Yorkshire, designed by Piet Oudolf. They will be cut back in the spring.

habitats for wildlife. Knowing when to deadhead and when to cut back foliage for regrowth is also useful.

The following table outlines some of the general management tasks to be undertaken on a monthly basis. But this is just a guide and is not a substitute for observing the garden day by day, and intervening little and often. It is best to have a light touch approach – tweaking here and there, removing vegetation when absolutely necessary, pruning a branch back when it is in the way, seeing what works and what does not.

Table 22 General management tasks

Throughout the year
Winter and early spring • Prune trees – remove any dead, diseased, crossing or damaged branches. **Spring, summer and autumn** • Keep ground weed free, especially around new trees. • Plants that self-seed can be selectively removed before they set seed – these may be classed as weeds but can also be more ornamental self-seeding species. • Ensure any new trees do not dry out. **Summer** • Deadhead roses to encourage repeat flowering but do not deadhead those with attractive hips such as *Rosa glauca*, *Rosa rugosa* or *Rosa canina*. • Mow lawn with high blades or just mow a path through it. **Autumn** • Clear leaves on lawn, paths and gravel areas only.
Monthly tasks
January
• Prune/cut back/train climbers depending on their requirements. • Cut back any soggy vegetation.
February
• Prune shrubs, depending on pruning group. • Prune/cut back/train climbers depending on their requirements. • Cut back old and dead growth on perennials, grasses and ferns as new growth appears. • Prune roses.

March
• Clear dead leaves. • Prune shrubs, depending on pruning group. • Apply a general fertiliser for shrubs if required. • Apply a rose fertiliser for roses. • Divide perennials and grasses. • Cut back old and dead growth on perennials, grasses and ferns as new growth appears. • Plant new perennials, grasses and ferns. • Apply mulch around all plants on damp soil. Do not cover crown of plant. • Sow annuals under glass.
April
• Check tree ties and stakes. • Feed trees. • Apply mulch around all plants on damp soil. Do not cover crown of plant. • Prune shrubs, depending on pruning group. • Apply a general fertiliser for shrubs if required. • Apply a rose fertiliser for roses. • Plant new perennials, grasses and ferns. • Stake tall perennials. • Deadhead bulbs. • Sow annuals under glass. • Pull up hardy annuals that have seeded into places where they are not wanted.
May
• Prune shrubs, depending on pruning group. • Stake tall perennials. • Deadhead bulbs. • Leave the lawn to grow longer to encourage wildflowers. • Sow annuals outside. • Pull up hardy annuals that have seeded into places where they are not wanted. • Plant bulbs 'in the green'.

Table 22 (Cont'd)

June
• Deadhead bulbs.
• Remove dead foliage from bulbs.
• Some perennials such as *Alchemilla* can be cut back after flowering to encourage new growth – the 'Chelsea Chop'.
• Thin out self-sown annuals.
• Pinch out the leading shoots on taller perennials when they reach 60cm in height to allow them to bush out and encourage flowering.

July
• Remove dead foliage from bulbs.
• Some perennials such as *Alchemilla* can be cut back after flowering to encourage new growth.
• Pinch out the leading shoots on taller perennials when they reach 60cm in height to allow them to bush out and encourage flowering.
• Prune plum trees if necessary.

August
• Deadhead any perennials and grasses which may seed themselves around too freely.
• Prune apple and pear trees to reduce size.

September
• Transplant perennials and plant new shrubs.
• Order bulbs.
• Deadhead any perennials and grasses which may seed themselves around too freely.
• Divide perennials (not grasses).
• Sow hardy annuals.

October
• Prune or cut back climbers depending on their requirements.
• Transplant perennials and plant new shrubs.
• Apply mulch around all plants on damp soil. Do not cover crown of plant.
• Sow hardy annuals.

November
• Prune/cut back/train climbers depending on their requirements.
• Plant bulbs for spring flowering.
• Cut back any soggy vegetation.

December
• Plan for the new year.

Pruning for Structure and Form

Pruning techniques can be used as a design tool to: divide up the space both horizontally and vertically; bring seasonal interest; create accents and focal points; provide frames and backdrops or to add an element of excitement and quirkiness to the garden. The time to prune, clip and train will depend on the species.

Evergreen hedges can be clipped to formal rectilinear shapes or into swirling waves and more elaborate topiary. They can be used as contrasting frames to dynamic and ephemeral species, the final height being determined by the aesthetics of the surrounding planting. Or they can be designed as screens and dividers between spaces in the garden, determining access routes and introducing an element of mystery.

Designers Patrick and Sylvie Quibel's quirkily pruned hedges at the *Jardin Plume* in France.

A clipped hedge frames the mass of perennials glimpsed beyond and the pruning echoes the pitch of the roof line and rusting arches at *Le Jardin Plume* designed by Patrick and Sylvie Quibel.

A cloud pruned tree among the hot springs in Beppu, Japan (© Rosemary Lee).

Coppicing, pollarding and creating multi-stemmed trees are all ways of creating different forms that contribute to the seasonal interest of the garden (*see* Chapter 5). Cloud pruning and pruning to lift the crown can be added to the list of techniques. The former is a Japanese method known as *niwaki*, and, as the name suggests, the aim is to create branches and foliage that look like clouds around a main trunk. It is suitable for evergreen species such as box, yew, pine and Japanese privet and the RHS has advice on how to create your own specimen. They also suggest trying this technique with Chilean myrtle (*Luma apiculata*), *Ilex crenata* and *Osmanthus* × *burkwoodii* (RHS, n.d.-d). The Chilean myrtle is particularly interesting for the seasonal successional garden, as it has scented white flowers and unusual, cinnamon-brown peeling bark.

Raising the crown of a tree or shrub can be carried out to create more of a see-through effect and to also allow for planting beneath the branches to extend the season of interest (RHS, n.d.-f). Choose a plant that has interesting main branches starting low to the ground and then remove the smaller side branches, gradually progressing up the trunks and frequently standing back to see how the tree looks from all angles. This technique can be undertaken with many species, both evergreen and deciduous: a few suggestions include *Sorbus* × *intermedia, Osmanthus* × *burkwoodii, Betula nigra, Viburnum rhytidophyllum* and *Pittosporum*. It is even possible to use a similar technique with some perennials, removing a few lower leaves to allow light through to smaller plants beneath.

Finally, there is the technique of pleaching where branches are pruned and tied in to a horizontal or vertical structure, creating stilt hedges for screening or overhead structures with parasol (roof-form) trees. Pleaching lends itself to more formal settings and allows you to introduce trees into a smaller space,

These parasol mulberry trees will grow to create a secluded seating area in this garden, designed by Alex Johnson (© Alex Johnson).

leaving more opportunities for additional planting to extend the season. A high pleached hedge lets in the sun and the ground beneath can be planted with low clipped shrubs and colourful perennials, whereas parasol trees introduce dappled shade and are suitable for underplanting with low-growing species that thrive in woodland habitats. Alternatively, they can be designed to provide shade over a seating area.

There are many examples of trees suitable for pleaching hedges, including beech and hornbeam, which will keep their leaves over the winter. Ornamental crab apples, lime, *Acer campestre* 'Elegant', *Liquidambar styraciflua*, fruitless mulberry and *Pyrus* 'Chanticleer' are just a few examples of trees that can be trained into a parasol form.

Combining Intensive and Extensive Maintenance

In traditional horticulture, plants are treated as individuals to be provided with ideal growing conditions that meet their specific requirements.

They are watered and fertilised, staked and deadheaded, divided when necessary and not encouraged to self-seed; this is called intensive maintenance. In Chapter 4, I discussed naturalistic planting and the interlacing approach to planting design. These sorts of plantings, in contrast with more traditional schemes, consider plants as communities and thus maintenance takes place at the level of the group, or even the whole planting bed – extensive maintenance. In the case of a meadow or a completely naturalistic scheme comprising only perennials and grasses, this involves cutting back all the vegetation at one time: either in the autumn for perennial meadows or in spring for steppe or prairie-style planting.

However, in the case of the mixed borders containing both shrubs and perennials that form the majority of gardens in this book, a combination of the intensive and extensive approach needs to be taken. This is also a more suitable way of managing a garden for wildlife, as it can be adapted to ensure there is shelter and food through the winter months. The skill is to know when to cut back, what to keep and what to remove.

This garden designed by the author uses a mix of extensive and intensive maintenance giving it a semi-naturalistic aesthetic.

An interlacing mass of perennials at John Little's garden takes an extensive approach to management, but there is still a need to weed little and often throughout the growing season.

Self-Seeding

It is not always possible to predict which perennials, annuals or grasses will self-seed; it depends on the conditions as well as the species. The gardener needs to be able to identify the different seedlings and remove those that they consider weeds, while leaving the more desirable species. As I discussed in Chapter 4, it may be easier to collect seed from annuals and either germinate it in pots or scatter it in the defined area in which you want the plants to grow. If certain species are allowed to randomly self-seed, they can provide

Blue, yellow and orange dots of colour from self-seeded *Centaurea montana* and *Meconopsis cambrica* interlace through the planting around this feature pot.

attractive dots of colour running through the more static planting, but there is also a risk that they will take over. Sometimes species seed into the centre of a low shrub or a cluster of perennials, resulting in the whole group having to be dug up and replanted. However, some self-seeding species, especially those that have winter flowers, are useful in a successional garden. *Helleborus foetidus* can happily seed itself around, turning up on the edge of gravel paths or in shady spots where little else will grow. Snowdrops may appear around the bases of tree trunks and under shrubs and hedges, as do cyclamen and tiny violets, adding winter interest among the bare branches. Cowslips and primroses are both happy to self-seed in sun and semi-shade and bring colour, and scent in the case of the primroses, in spring. Other self-seeders have a long period of interest: *Verbena bonariensis* continues to flower into the autumn and the low-growing grass, *Milium effusum* 'Aureum', adds splashes of bright yellow-green to shady places.

Dead Leaves, Seedheads and Stems

As I have stressed throughout this book, is not necessary or desirable to cut back all dead and dying foliage and seedheads in the garden: rather, embrace these signs of the changing seasons and provide habitats for wildlife at the same time. However, where the spent foliage becomes unsightly – a damp, brown mass of vegetation – some judicious clearing and cutting back can be undertaken. Some grasses look good well into

Calamagrostis x *acutiflora* 'Overdam' stands tall through the winter in this garden at the Manor House, Stevington, Bedfordshire, designed by Kathy Brown (© MMGI/ Marianne Majerus).

the winter, but make sure that the dead flower and seed stems are removed in late February or early March just as the green, new growth appears. Deciduous ferns die back completely leaving dead fronds to protect the crown and, at some point in late winter, these can be removed. It depends on how unsightly they are. Evergreen ferns, although structural and handsome over the winter, benefit from tidying up in spring and the older leaves removed. Exposing the new growth allows us to appreciate the furry, brown shuttlecocks as they start to unfold. It also gives space for bulbs, especially snowdrops, to shine.

Competition

Schemes that practise extensive maintenance require an understanding of the relative competitiveness of the different plant species: if all the plants in a group are treated in the same way, there will be some that outcompete their neighbours when the conditions are more favourable for them. I have also pointed out that in the successional garden, competition can be a problem. When placing plants so that later in the year a taller species shades a lower-growing one, there is sometimes a danger that the latter does not get enough light or nutrients and suffers accordingly. Keeping a watchful eye on what is happening in the garden can help to pre-empt any problems; for example, it might be necessary to stake the taller perennials to prevent them leaning over other plants.

As I discussed in Chapter 6, reducing the fertility of the soil can prevent plants growing too tall and this is something to consider as part of the long-term planning for the garden. Biodegradable mulches such as compost, wood chip and leaf mould break down in the soil and help to improve its structure, add nutrients and retain water (RHS, n.d.-g), whereas the decorative aggregates – pebbles, slate, gravel – are not biodegradable and therefore do not increase the nutrient level.

The 'Chelsea Chop'

At the end of May some gardeners advocate undertaking what is colloquially called the 'Chelsea Chop' because it occurs at the same time as the UK Chelsea Flower Show (Crozier, 2022). Established herbaceous perennials can put on new growth rapidly as the soil heats up and quickly become leggy and need staking. Cutting them back by a third or a half to about 30cm from the ground encourages them to bush out and can also delay the display of flowers. Flowers may be smaller on plants treated in this way, but the increased bushiness means that they will probably be more abundant. In order to increase the length of the flowering period, leave some plants and cut back others, or only cut back selected stems on an individual plant (Crozier, 2022).

As I pointed out in Chapter 6, John Little takes the idea of a summer cut back even further by mowing different sections of his garden at different times to encourage a longer flowering period. This results in flowers of the same species just emerging in one part of the garden when they may be nearly over in another. It is also worth noting that plants cope better in drought conditions if they are pruned in spring or early summer (Bower, 2021).

The Beth Chatto Nursery gives a list of perennials suitable for this treatment including *Achillea*, *Aster*, *Helenium*, *Helianthus*, *Penstemon*, *Rudbeckia* and upright forms of *Hylotelephium* (Crozier, 2022) (RHS, n.d.-c). I have also tried this with *Hydrangea* 'Annabelle' to prevent the stems falling over under the weight of the large flowers. It is worth noting that the 'Chelsea Chop' may not be so effective in the north of the UK where the growing season is shorter.

Detailed Management for the College Garden

The following table gives detailed information for the management of some of the plants in the college garden discussed in Chapter 3, optimised for seasonal succession.

The beginning of autumn in the college garden, designed by the author. (With special thanks to the Provost and Fellows of The Queen's College.)

Table 23 Detailed management schedule

TREES	Pruning not necessary. Remove any dead or dying branches if required. If necessary, a branch of a multi-stemmed tree, such as *Amelanchier*, can be taken back to the ground. *See* Chapter 5.
APPLES Beckley Red Oxford Hoard Winter Greening	Fan train along wall (*see* below). Prune and train in late winter/early spring. Tie in selected branches as they grow over the summer. Remove any unwanted branches as they grow over the summer. Remove fruit for first two years. Use codling moth traps in late spring/early summer.
CLIMBERS AND WALL SHRUBS	
Chaenomeles × *superba* 'Pink Lady' *Osmanthus delavayi*	Fan train along wall (*see* below). Remove unwanted shoots when necessary.
Clematis 'Polish Spirit' (group 3)	In early spring cut back the previous year's stems to a pair of strong buds about 15–20cm above ground level.
Pyracantha 'Saphyr Red'	Flowers mainly on shoots produced the previous year. When pruning try to retain as much two-year-old wood as possible. Prune hard to wall and train. Retain berries for birds. Do not allow to get out of shape.
Rosa 'Ghislaine de Féligonde' (rambler)	Prune in late summer, after show of flowers and hips. Can be deadheaded. Retain hips where possible. Renovation can be carried out at any time between late autumn and late winter.
Rosa 'Gloire de Dijon' (climber) *R.* 'Madame Alfred Carrière' (climber) *R.* 'Tess of the d'Urbervilles' (climber)	Deadhead to encourage repeat flowering. Prune in late autumn or in winter, after the flowers have faded. Tie in to wires on wall to create fan shape.
Wisteria sinensis	Prune twice a year, in July or August and January or February. Cut back the whippy green shoots of the current year's growth to five or six leaves after flowering. Cut back the same growths to two or three buds in January or February.
SHRUBS	
Berberis wilsoniae	Prune lightly to maintain shape after flowering. Try to retain berries.
Buxus sempervirens	Apply nematodes during the growing season to protect from box moth caterpillar. Trim to shape in August/September. If clipped surface becomes crowded on top of hedge, remove some of the growing shoots by clipping 30cm below the surface.
Cornus sanguinea 'Midwinter Fire'	Prune hard every one to three years for stem colour. Use coppicing techniques (*see* Chapter 5).
Corylus avellana 'Zellernus'	Prune out a proportion of the stems to the ground. Or use coppicing techniques and cut back completely every few years (*see* Chapter 5).
Cotinus 'Grace'	Prune lightly in early spring if required to maintain shape. Can respond to coppicing in March.
Hydrangea 'Annabelle'	Prune if required after flowering but better to keep the dead flower heads over the winter. Cut back in spring to about 30–40cm from the ground to encourage new growth and keep in shape.

Table 23 (*Cont'd*)

PERENNIALS	The general principle with perennials and grasses is to leave the dead flower heads on over the winter to provide structure and habitats for wildlife. If the plant begins to look unsightly it can be cut back as required. Otherwise, they should be cut back in early spring before the new growth begins. The timing of this will depend on the new growth. A few special cases are detailed below.
Echinacea purpurea 'Magnus Superior' *Echinacea purpurea* 'White Swan'	Leave flower heads over winter. Cut back in early spring. Can respond to cutting back at the end of May, but make sure all the flower heads are kept for the winter.
Epimedium × *rubrum*	Cut back all the leaves in early spring before the tiny flower stems appear. Be careful not to cut the flowers as they are very delicate.
Euphorbia characias wulfenii *Euphorbia robbiae* 'Purpurea'	Leave flower heads until they become unsightly and then cut back to the base avoiding new growth. Warning: skin irritant.
Helleborus foetidus	Remove dead flower heads when they become unsightly in midsummer. Remove any dead leaves as necessary. To avoid self-seeding, remove flower heads earlier.
Helleborus orientalis	Remove dead flower heads after flowering. Cut back leaves to base in late autumn/early winter to allow the flowers to be seen.
Phlomis russeliana	Leave flower heads over winter. Cut back in early spring. May self-seed and can be difficult to remove.
GRASSES	If seeding becomes a problem cutting back may need to be earlier. In my experience, these grasses do not self-seed except perhaps the *Calamagrostis brachytricha*. However, this has beautiful flower heads which last throughout the winter.
Calamagrostis brachytricha	Leave flower heads throughout the winter and only cut back in early March when the tips of new growth are visible.
Calamagrostis × *acutiflora* 'Karl Foerster'	Leave flower heads throughout the winter and only cut back in March. Careful of new growth
Deschampsia cespitosa 'Bronzeschleier'	Cut back dead seedheads when they become unsightly.
FERNS	
Asplenium scolopendrium Cristatum group	Allow old leaves to protect crown over winter before removing in spring.
Athyrium niponicum var. *pictum*	Cut back dead and unsightly leaves in winter.
Polystichum setiferum 'Dahlem' *Polystichum setiferum* 'Proliferum'	Cut back dead and unsightly leaves in early spring. Avoid the fronds of new growth.
BULBS	
Allium 'Purple Sensation' *Camassia leichtlinii caerulea* *Nectaroscordum siculum*	Leave flower heads until they become unsightly, probably around June/July. Allow leaves to die back before removing.
Crocus tommasinianus 'Whitewell Purple', *C.* × *angustifolius* 'Janis Ruksans'	Do not mow grass until crocus leaves have died back.

Clipped yew hedges frame the feathery plumes of *Calamagrostis brachytricha*. (With special thanks to the Provost and Fellows of The Queen's College.)

Training Wall Shrubs and Trees

Apples, pears and stone fruit, such as cherries, gages, plums and damsons, all lend themselves to training along walls and fences. This has a functional purpose – it ensures the fruit is produced at a height that is easy for us to reach and takes up less space than a full-grown tree. There are three distinctive shapes – cordons, fans and espaliers – all of which are trained flat against a vertical surface or support. Espaliers consist of a vertical stem from which extend tiers of horizontal branches, maybe three or four in all. Apples and pears trained in this way can eventually reach 3-4m in width and 1.8m high (RHS, n.d.-a). Fan-trained trees are similar in size but with a short vertical stem, about 30-40cm in height, and with branches radiating out in a fan shape from the top of the

stem (RHS, n.d.-e). Trees trained at a 45-degree angle are known as cordons and take up less space than espaliers or fans: they can be planted as little as 60cm apart (RHS, n.d.-b).

All forms of training require a strong supporting structure from the outset, and it is important to remember that the ground at the base of a fence or wall is usually dry and in a rain shadow, so plant the tree about 40cm away from the support and check it does not dry out.

Fan and espalier training can be applied to other wall shrubs, although perhaps not in quite such a regimented fashion as with the fruit trees. *Pyracantha* 'Orange Glow' is a good candidate for a formal espalier and this is also a way to keep this vigorous plant in check. It can be pruned

Top: Espaliered apple trees frame a path in a community orchard in Broomfield Park in London. Left: This *Chaenomeles* has been pruned and trained to provide a high canopy of flowers above the windows in a small front garden.

to make the berries more visible, thus providing a touch of colour and interest in the winter. Other wall shrubs include *Osmanthus burkwoodii, Osmanthus delavayi, Chaenomeles, Itea ilicifolia* and *Garrya elliptica* 'James Roof'.

In the successional garden, the advantages of training trees and wall shrubs are twofold. Aesthetically, these forms are a delight throughout the year, even in winter, especially if you are lucky enough to have the textural qualities of an old wall as a backdrop. They also take up less space, allowing layers of lower-growing perennials to be planted in the foreground.

An immaculately clipped dome of yew acts as a punctuation point beside this rusting gate at *Le Jardin d'Agapanthe*, Normandy, designed by Alexandre Thomas.

Longevity

In any garden that aims to be sustainable it is clearly important to consider the longevity of shrubs and trees and to take account of life expectancy when selecting perennials. Including a percentage of longer-lived species ensures the garden continues to provide interest over time; in a design, shorter-lived plants can be thought of as acting as companions to their longer-lived neighbours, maybe filling gaps before shrubs reach their mature size.

We use the terms annual, biennial, perennial and even ephemeral to describe plant behaviour but, in fact, these definitions are fairly arbitrary: biennials may survive for more than two years and not all perennials are long-lived. As Noel Kingsbury points out 'realising that not all perennials are truly perennial is very important for the long-term development of planting design' (2013: p.28). Coming full circle and returning to the ideas of Chapter 1, we can get some idea of how plants will behave by observing their wild counterparts. Many of the shorter-lived species that we use in our gardens originate from habitats that are subject to change and instability. Examples are *Aquilegia* and *Digitalis* that grow on the woodland edge or take advantage of sudden changes in light levels as trees are felled.

Grassland plants such as *Knautia* may also be short-lived due to the need to cope with disturbance by grazing animals (Kingsbury, 2013). These species are often the ones that self-seed in our gardens.

Kingsbury suggests several perennials that will survive for years including *Epimedium* × *perralchicum*, *Anemone* × *hybrida* and *Baptisia australis*, but points out that the latter two species take a while to establish. He also notes that different varieties of the same genus may have different life spans: *Echinacea purpurea* is fairly short-lived whereas *E. pallida*, although slow to establish, is much longer-lived (Kingsbury, 2013). Other examples of species that have the potential to thrive year after year include *Acanthus mollis* 'Rue Ledon', *Veronicastrum virginicum*, *Origanum* 'Herrenhausen' and *Hylotelephium* 'Herbstfreude' (Brockbank, 2017). However, we should be aware that as the climate changes, these behaviours may be affected.

Competition can also play a part in determining which species will survive in the long term; even the most resilient plants can be overwhelmed by a more vigorous neighbour. Often cultivars tend to have a shorter lifespan (von Schoenaich, 1994) and nutrient stress (as found in gardens planted on mineral substrates) is another factor, resulting in slower growth and a corresponding longer lifespan – a moderate amount of stress can be beneficial (Hitchmough, 1994). When deciding on a management regime, we should consider how to reduce the nutrient additions to the minimum needed to produce healthy, aesthetically pleasing plants.

Although we can do our best to plant with longevity in mind, change is something that gardeners, garden owners and designers are always cognisant of: in some cases, we try to keep it at bay, but in others we embrace it, revelling in the drama and excitement. Perhaps the most useful thing to remember when creating and maintaining a garden is the importance of observation, of noticing the changes – spotting when plants need a helping hand, learning from what is happening around us, taking account of new research. In this way we can continue to manage our gardens effectively for ourselves, for the plants and for the wildlife.

AFTERWORD

Throughout this book I have shown how we can create planting schemes that bring joy and delight through the seasons, while also balancing this with the need to consider the sustainability of our designs and to ensure that both humans and wildlife can benefit. Gardens are always changing – houses are sold, owners move on, management regimes are not followed, and we all love to keep adding beautiful plants where there is probably no more space.

Whether we choose a planting design with a traditional aesthetic or prefer a more naturalistic approach, we can still focus on sustainability, exploring different ways of planting, using mineral substrates, mulching, taking the no-dig approach, sourcing locally, planting for diversity and much more.

With more extreme weather events and a climate in crisis, we need to be open to researching new species with resilience in mind, examining changes in behaviour of our favourite garden plants and of those in the world around us, learning from each other, noticing what is happening from day to day and taking a 'little and often' approach to management. These are just a few of the things that can help to ensure that our gardens continue to delight throughout the seasons and over the years, while also becoming part of a potentially huge resource to help improve our environment.

Spring flowers beneath an olive in Crete (© Sergio Denche).

Habitat posts run through a mass of interlacing perennials and shrubs in the RSPB garden designed by the author with Alex Johnson (© MMGI/Marianne Majerus).

BIBLIOGRAPHY

Agroforestry Research Trust (n.d.) *Forest gardening.* Online, Agroforestry Research Trust. Available from: https://www.agroforestry.co.uk/about-agroforestry/forest-gardening/ [Accessed 12/3/2023].

Architectural Plants (2023a) *Eucalyptus pauciflora subsp. debeuzevillei.* Online, Architectural Plants. Available from: https://www.architecturalplants.com/product/eucalyptus-debeuzevillei/ [Accessed 1/3/2023].

Architectural Plants (2023b) *Pinus mugo 'Mughus'.* Online, Architectural Plants. Available from: https://www.architecturalplants.com/product/pinus-mugo-mugo/ [Accessed 1/3/2023].

Architectural Plants (n.d.) *Lyonothamnus floribundus asplenifolius.* Online, Architectural Plants. Available from: https://www.architecturalplants.com/product/lyonothamnus-floribundus-aspleniifolius/ [Accessed 4/4/2023].

Bailey, R. & Wilkinson, R. (2023) Sustainability in garden design – the next steps. *Garden Design Journal,* Jan/Feb (243), pp. 37–39.

Basson, H. (2019) *Olivier Filippi's Dry Garden Delights.* Online, Garden Design Journal. Available from: https://www.sgd.org.uk/garden_design_journal/features/231/olivier_filippis_dry_garden_delights/ [Accessed 23/4/2023].

Basson, H. & Basson, J. (2017) Climate Change Plants: Drier. *Garden Design Journal,* Sept. (182), pp. 23–26.

BD Editors (2019) *Ecological Succession.* Online, Biology Dictionary. Available from: https://biologydictionary.net/ecological-succession/ [Accessed 15/19/2022].

Beth Chatto's plants and gardens (n.d.) *Eurybia divaricata.* Online, Beth Chatto's Plants and Gardens. Available from: https://www.bethchatto.co.uk/a-z/e-h/eurybia/aster-divaricatus.htm [Accessed 25/3/2023].

Bower, S. (2021) *Nature Rising from the Rubble, RHS Bursary Study Tour.* Online, RHS. Available from: https://www.rhs.org.uk/education-learning/pdf/bursaries/Bursary-Reports/rhs-bursary-report-sally-bower.pdf [Accessed 12/4/2023].

Brockbank, J. (2017) Enduring Love, *Garden Design Journal,* July (180), pp. 27–30.

Bruce, J. (2020) *Olivier and Clara Filippi's Le Jardin Sec: a windswept, Mediterranean gravel garden.* Online, Gardens Illustrated. Available from: https://www.gardensillustrated.com/gardens/international/jardin-sec-filippi-gravel-garden-france/ [Accessed 27/4/2023].

Bruce, J. (n.d.) *Four Drought-tolerant Planting Combinations from Olivier and Clara Filippi's*

Garden in France. Online, Gardens Illustrated. Available from: https://www.gardensillustrated. com/plants/planting-ideas/drought-tolerant-planting-combinations/ [Accessed 27/4/2023].

Buglife (n.d.) *Identifying Open Mosaic Habitat*. Online, Buglife. Available from: https://cdn.buglife.org. uk/2020/01/Identifying-open-mosaic-habitat.pdf [Accessed 22/6/2021].

Butterfly conservation (n.d.) *Caterpillar Foodplants*. Online, Butterfly conservation. Available from: https://butterfly-conservation.org/moths/why-moths-matter/about-moths/caterpillar-foodplants [Accessed 6/4/2021].

Cameron, R., Brindley, P., Mears, M., McEwan, K., Ferguson, F., Sheffield, D., Jorgensen, A., Riley, J., Goodrick, J., Ballard, L. & Richardson, M. (2020) Where the wild things are! Do urban green spaces with greater avian biodiversity promote more positive emotions in humans? *Urban Ecosystems,* 23 (2), pp. 301–317.

Chalker-Scott, L. (2019) *Do black walnuts have allelopathic effects on other plants?* Online, Washington State University. Available from: https://rex.libraries.wsu.edu/esploro/outputs/report/Do-black-walnut-trees-have-allelopathic/99900501686101842#file-0 [Accessed 23/4/2023].

Champion, H. (2014) *The History of the Nuttery*. Online, Sissinghurst Castle. Available from: https://sissinghurstcastle.wordpress.com/2014/05/08/the-history-of-the-nuttery/ [Accessed 1/5/2023].

Chatto, B. *The Dry Garden*, (Weidenfeld & Nicholson, 1978).

Climate positive design (2023) *Design for our future: Be climate positive*. Online, Climate positive design. Available from: https://climatepositivedesign.com [Accessed 23/2/2023].

Crawford, M. (2014) What is forest gardening? *Garden Design Journal,* Sept (146), pp. 27–29.

Crocus (n.d.) *Long flowering plants for your garden*. Online, Crocus. Available from: https://www.crocus.co.uk/features/_/articleid.1502/ [Accessed 7/3/2023].

Crowe, S. & Mitchell, M. (1988) *The pattern of landscape*. Chichester: Packard Publishing.

Crozier, L. (2022) *The Chelsea Chop - How To Do It*. Online, Beth Chatto Gardens. Available from: https://www.bethchatto.co.uk/discover/our-blog/guides/the-chelsea-chop-how-to-do-it.htm [Accessed 22/2/2023].

Department of Agriculture Environment and Rural Affairs (n.d.) *Integrated Pest Management*. Online, Department of Agriculture, Environment and Rural Affairs. Available from: https://www.daera-ni.gov. uk/articles/integrated-pest-management [Accessed 12/3/2023].

Doick, K. (2023) *Influence of vegetation on pollutant pathways*. Online, Forest research. Available from: https://www.forestresearch.gov.uk/research/influence-of-vegetation-on-pollutant-pathways/ [Accessed 12/72023].

Dowding, C. (2018) *Organic gardening: The natural no-dig way.* Cambridge: Green Books.

Doxiadis, T. (n.d.) *Development of 30 villas in Antiparos, Greece*. Online, Doxiadis+. Available from: https://doxiadisplus.com/landscapes-of-cohabitation-on-antiparos-island/ [Accessed 12/4/2023].

Dusoir, R. (2019) *Planting the Ourdolf gardens at Hauser and Wirth Somerset*. UK: Hauser & Wirth Publishers / Filbert Press.

English Partnerships (2006) *The Brownfield Guide: a practitioner's guide to land reuse in England.* London: English Partnerships Dept. for Communities and Local Government.

Filippi, O. (2018) *Beth Chatto Symposium: Olivier Filippi Mediterranean Landscapes as inspiration for planting design*. Online, Beth Chatto's Plants and Gardens. Available from: https://www.youtube. com/watch?v=CEdigaE6ck8 [Accessed 24/4/2023].

Filippi, O. (2019) *Bringing the Mediterranean Into Your Garden: How to Capture the Natural Beauty of the Mediterranean Garrigue.* UK: Filbert Press.

Garden Organic (2021) *The No-Dig method*. Online, Garden Organic. Available from: https://www. gardenorganic.org.uk/no-dig-method [Accessed 12/10/2021].

Gardeners' World (2021) *Repeat-flowering perennials to grow*. Online, Gardeners' World Magazine. Available from: https://www.gardenersworld.com/how-to-grow-plants/repeat-flowering-perennials-to-grow/ [Accessed 7/3/2023].

Gardeners' World (n.d.) *Native pond plants*. Online, Gardeners' World. Available from: https://www. gardenersworld.com/plants/native-plants-for-wildlife-ponds/ [Accessed 16/5/2021].

Gardens Illustrated (n.d.) *24 key plants from Piet Oudolf's field at Hauser and Wirth art gallery and garden in Somerset*. Online, Gardens Illustrated.

Available from: https://www.gardensillustrated.com/gardens/24-key-plants-from-the-garden-at-hauser-and-wirth-art-gallery-in-somerset/ [Accessed 14/1/2023].

Gaston, K. J., Smith, R. M., Thompson, K. & Warren, P. H. (2005) Urban domestic gardens (II): experimental tests of methods for increasing biodiversity. *Biodiversity & Conservation,* 14 (2), pp. 395–413.

Glanville, R. (2019) *Zanthoxylum simulans.* Online, Gardeners' World. Available from: https://www.gardenersworld.com/plants/zanthoxylum-simulans/ [Accessed 20/6/2023].

Goulson, D. (2020) Honey Traps. *Garden Design Journal,* November (220), pp. 21-24.

Greenbee landscapes (2019) *Piet Oudolf.* Online, Greenbee landscapes. Available from: https://www.greenbee-landscapes.co.uk/2019/02/25/piet-oudolf/ [Accessed 13/1/2023].

Grime, J. P. (2002) *Plant strategies and vegetation processes.* Chichester: John Wiley.

Hansen, R. & Stahl, F., *Perennials and their Garden Habitats,* (Cambridge University Press 1993).

Heath, O. (2022) *Chelsea Flower Show: Monty Don says 'two things bother him' about the Rewilding Britain Landscape garden.* Online, House Beautiful. Available from: https://www.housebeautiful.com/uk/garden/a40126888/chelsea-flower-show-monty-don-rewilding-britain-garden/ [Accessed 21/7/2023].

Heatherington, C., Buried Narratives. In: A. Jorgensen & R. Keenan (Eds.) *Urban Wildscapes* (Routledge, 2012) pp. 171–186.

Heatherington, C., *Reimagining Industrial Sites: Changing Histories and Landscapes,* (Routledge, 2018).

Heatherington, C., *Revealing Change in Cultural Landscapes: Material, Spatial and Ecological Considerations* (Routledge, 2021).

Heatherington, C. & Johnson, A., *Habitat Creation in Garden Design: A Guide to Designing Places for People and Wildlife* (The Crowood Press, 2022).

Heatherington, C., Jorgensen, A. & Walker, S. (2017) Understanding landscape change in a former brownfield site. *Landscape Research,* 44 (1), pp. 19–34.

Heatherington, C. & Sargeant, J. *A New Naturalism* (Packard Publishing Ltd., now Liverpool University Press, 2005).

Hitchmough, J. (1994) Natural neighbours. *Landscape Design,* 229, pp. 16–22.

Hitchmough, J. (2020) *Thinking the unthinkable: designing with plants in an era of rapid climate change.* online: SGD Digital Autumn Conference 2020.

Hitchmough, J. & Livingstone, M. (2020) No fines please. *Landscape Journal,* 1, pp. 22–26.

Hoffman, J. (2013) *Five Great Grasses from the Oudolf Garden.* Online, Hoffman Nursery. Available from: https://hoffmannursery.com/blog/article/five-great-grasses-from-the-oudolf-garden [Accessed 14/1/2023].

House and Garden (n.d.) *The enchanting autumn landscape of Piet Oudolf's garden at Hauser & Wirth Somerset.* Online, House and Garden. Available from: https://www.houseandgarden.co.uk/gallery/piet-oudolfs-garden-at-hauser-wirth-somerset [Accessed 14/3/2023].

Hunt, L. (2023) Rising from the rubble. *The Garden,* (March), pp. 51–58.

Jones, L. (2011) The pioneer spirit. *Garden Design Journal,* May (106), pp. 27–32.

Kelly, J., *The All Seasons Garden* (Frances Lincoln Ltd, 1987).

King, C. M., Robinson, J. S. & Cameron, R. W. (2012) Flooding tolerance in four 'Garrigue' landscape plants: implications for their future use in the urban landscapes of north-west Europe? *Landscape and Urban Planning,* 107 (2), pp. 100–110.

Kingsbury, N. (2013) Long-term plant performance, part 1 longevity. *Garden Design Journal,* March, pp. 27–29.

Korn, P. (2018) *The Beth Chatto Symposium - Designing for plants.* Online, Beth Chatto's Plants & Gardens. Available from: https://www.youtube.com/watch?v=mv2MUJdBamA [Accessed 23/4/2023].

Lacey, S. (1995) Steppe into the garden. *Garden Design Journal,* 2 (2).

Lloyd, C., *The Well Tempered Garden* (HarperCollins, 1970).

Lloyd, C. (2004) Perpetual motion. *The Guardian,* 13th March.

Lloyd, C., *A Lifetime of Seasons: The Best of Christopher Lloyd* (Weidenfeld & Nicholson, 2021).

Midgley, D. (2018) *Stars of the Grasslands Garden.* Online, Horniman Museum and Gardens. Available from: https://www.horniman.ac.uk/story/stars-of-the-grasslands-garden/ [Accessed 24/4/2023].

Mogendorff, M. & Romain, C., *How to Grow the Flowers* (Pavilion, 2022).

Nassauer, J. (1995) Messy ecosystems, orderly frames. *Landscape Journal,* 14 (2), pp. 161–170.

National Trust (n.d.) *What is coppicing?* Online, National Trust. Available from: https://www. nationaltrust.org.uk/discover/nature/trees-plants/ what-is-coppicing [Accessed 2/3/2023].

Oudolf, P. & Kingsbury, N., *Designing with plants* (Conran Octopus Ltd, 1999).

Pearson, D. (2018) *The Beth Chatto Symposium - Dan Pearson Emulating Nature in the public arena.* Online, Beth Chatto's Plants & Gardens. Available from: https://www.youtube.com/ watch?v=MKhgQ_ei2Tk [Accessed 23/4/2023].

Plantlife (2017) *Road verges: last refuge for some of our rarest flowers and plants.* Online, Plantlife. Available from: https://www.plantlife.org.uk/ application/files/4514/9261/2387/Road_verges_ report_19_April_FINAL.pdf [Accessed 27/10/2022].

Plantlife (n.d.-a) *How to mow your lawn for wild flowers.* Online, Plantlife. Available from: https:// nomowmay.plantlife.org.uk/what-is-no-mow- may/wild-flower-lawn/ [Accessed 12/3/2023].

Plantlife (n.d.-b) *Road verges: 20 per cent drop in diversity of wild flowers puts bees at risk as plant 'marauders' take over.* Online, Plantlife. Available from: https://www.plantlife.org.uk/uk/about-us/ news/road-verge-marauders [Accessed 27/20/2022].

Plantlife (n.d.-c) *Why we need to keep peat in the ground – and out of our gardens.* Online, Plantlife. Available from: https://www.plantlife.org.uk/uk/ our-work/campaigning-change/why-we-need-to- keep-peat-in-the-ground-and-out-of-our-gardens [Accessed 2/1/2023].

Rafferty, J. P. (n.d.) *What Is the Difference Between Primary and Secondary Ecological Succession?* Online, Encyclopaedia Britannica Available from: https://www.britannica.com/science/ecological- succession [Accessed 15/10/2022].

Rainer, T. (2018) Planting renaissance. *Garden Design Journal,* August (193), pp. 25–28.

Rainer, T. & West, C., *Planting in a Post-Wild World: Designing Plant Communities for Resilient Landscapes* (Timber Press, 2015).

Rewilding Britain (2023) *Knepp Castle Estate.* Online, Rewilding Britain. Available from: https://www. rewildingbritain.org.uk/rewilding-projects/ knepp-castle-estate [Accessed 25/7/2023].

RHS (2021a) *Native and non-native plants for plant- dwelling invertebrates.* Online, RHS. Available from: https://www.rhs.org.uk/advice/profile?PID=1019 [Accessed 18 March 2021].

RHS (2021b) *RHS Plants for Pollinators.* Online, RHS. Available from: https://www.rhs.org.uk/science/ conservation-biodiversity/wildlife/plants-for- pollinators [Accessed 13/9/2021].

RHS (2021c) *Wildlife in gardens.* Online, RHS. Available from: https://www.rhs.org.uk/advice/ profile?PID=551 [Accessed 28/9/2021].

RHS (n.d.-a) *Apples and pears: espalier pruning and training.* Online, Royal Horticultural Society. Available from: https://www.rhs.org.uk/fruit/ apples/training-espalier [Accessed 23/2/2023].

RHS (n.d.-b) *Apples and pears: starting a new cordon.* Online, Royal Horticultural Society. Available from: https://www.rhs.org.uk/fruit/ apples/growing-and-training-as-cordons [Accessed 23/2/2023].

RHS (n.d.-c) *Chelsea chop.* Online, Royal Horticultural Society. Available from: https://www.rhs.org.uk/ pruning/chelsea-chop [Accessed 7/3/2023].

RHS (n.d.-d) *Cloud pruning.* Online, Royal Horticultural Society. Available from: https://www. rhs.org.uk/plants/types/trees/cloud-pruning [Accessed 23/2/2023].

RHS (n.d.-e) *Fan-trained trees: initial training.* Online, Royal Horticultural Society. Available from: https:// www.rhs.org.uk/fruit/fruit-trees/initial-fan-training [Accessed 23/2/2023].

RHS (n.d.-f) *Garden trends for 2021: clever ways to fit trees and shrubs into small gardens.* Online, Royal Horticultural Society. Available from: https://www. rhs.org.uk/garden-inspiration/design/how-to-fit- trees-and-shrubs-into-a-small-garden [Accessed 16/5/2023].

RHS (n.d.-g) *Mulches and mulching.* Online, Royal Horticultural Society. Available from: https://www. rhs.org.uk/soil-composts-mulches/mulch [Accessed 22/2/2023].

RHS (n.d.-h) *Trees for climate change.* Online, Royal Horticultural Society. Available from: https://www. rhs.org.uk/plants/types/trees/for-climate-change [Accessed 4/4/2023].

Rollings, R. (2018) *The 'June gap' – a tough time for bees?* Online, Rosybee. Available from: https:// www.rosybee.com/blog/2011/06/the-june-gap-a- tough-time-for-bees [Accessed 20/9/2021].

Rollings, R. (2019) *Six year research study*. Online, Rosybee. Available from: https://www.rosybee.com/research [Accessed 18 March 2021].

Rollings, R. & Goulson, D. (2019) Quantifying the attractiveness of garden flowers for pollinators. *Journal of Insect Conservation,* 23, pp. 803–817.

Salisbury, A., Al-Beidh, S., Armitage, J., Bird, S., Bostock, H., Platoni, A., Tatchell, M., Thompson, K. & Perry, J. (2017) Enhancing gardens as habitats for plant-associated invertebrates: should we plant native or exotic species? *Biodiversity and Conservation,* 26 (11), pp. 2657–2673.

Salisbury, A., Armitage, J., Bostock, H., Perry, J., Tatchell, M. & Thompson, K. (2015) Editor's Choice: Enhancing gardens as habitats for flower-visiting aerial insects (pollinators): should we plant native or exotic species? *Journal of Applied Ecology,* 52 (5), pp. 1156–1164.

Segall, B. (2022) Resilient trees. *Garden Design Journal,* October (240), pp. 27-31.

Society of Garden Designers (2022) *Manifesto for Sustainable Gardens & Landscapes*. Online, Society of Garden Designers. Available from: https://www.sgd.org.uk/_userfiles/pages/files/manifesto/manifesto_for_sustainable_garden_landscapes_image.jpeg [Accessed 2/1/2023].

The Royal Society for the Protection of Birds (n.d.) *Hedge history*. Online, RSPB. Available from: https://www.rspb.org.uk/our-work/conservation/conservation-and-sustainability/advice/conservation-land-management-advice/farm-hedges/history-of-hedgerows/ [Accessed 27/10/2022].

Thomas, H. (2008) Going up the wall. *Garden Design Journal,* Sept (74), pp. 25–27.

Thompson, J. N. (n.d.) *Ecological succession*. Online, Encyclopaedia Britannica Available from: https://www.britannica.com/science/ecological-succession [Accessed 15/10/2022].

Thompson, K. & Head, S. (2020) *Gardens as a resource for wildlife*. Online, Wildlife Gardening Forum. Available from: http://www.wlgf.org/The%20garden%20Resource.pdf [Accessed 28/9/2021].

Traverso, V. (2020) *The best trees to reduce air pollution*. Online, BBC. Available from: https://www.bbc.com/future/article/20200504-which-trees-reduce-air-pollution-best [Accessed 2/1/2023].

Tree, I., *Wilding: The return to nature of a British farm* (Picador, 2018).

Tree, I. (2023) *Don't be scared of rewilding, Monty Don and Alan Titchmarsh: it's a garden revelation*. Online, *The Guardian*. Available from: https://www.theguardian.com/commentisfree/2023/jul/24/rewilding-monty-don-alan-titchmarsh-garden [Accessed 24/7/2023].

University of Sheffield (2020) *Less flamboyant flowers are more resilient to climate chaos, research shows*. Online, University of Sheffield. Available from: https://www.sheffield.ac.uk/landscape/news/less-flamboyant-flowers-are-more-resilient-climate-chaos-research-shows [Accessed 28/12/2022].

Van Groeningen, I. (1995) Natural choices. *The Garden,* October 1995.

von Schoenaich, B. (1994) The end of the border? *Landscape Design,* 229, pp. 9–14.

Ward, R. (1989-90) Harmony in wild planting. *Landscape Design,* 186, pp. 30–32.

Webster, E. (2017) Climate change plants: extreme. *Garden Design Journal,* Oct. (183), pp. 23–36.

Webster, E., Cameron, R. W. F. & Culham, A., *Gardening in a Changing Climate* (Royal Horticultural Society, 2017).

Westhorpe, T. (2021) Breaking ground. *Garden Design Journal,* December (232), pp. 32–36.

Willaert (n.d.) *Climate trees*. Online, Willaert. Available from: https://www.willaert.be/en/inspiration-page/trends/climate-trees [Accessed 21/2/2023].

Woodland Trust (2013) *Hedges and hedgerows*. Online, Woodland Trust. Available from: https://www.woodlandtrust.org.uk/media/1808/hedges-and-hedgerows-position-statement.pdf [Accessed 25/9/2021].

Woodland Trust (n.d.) *Heathland and moorland*. Online, Woodland Trust. Available from: https://www.woodlandtrust.org.uk/trees-woods-and-wildlife/habitats/heathland-and-moorland/ [Accessed 29/10/2022].

WWT (n.d.) *A guide to native pond plants...what not to choose*. Online, WWT Wildfowl and Wetlands Trust. Available from: https://www.wwt.org.uk/discover-wetlands/gardening-for-wetlands/a-guide-to-native-pond-plants [Accessed 15/5/2021].

Ybern, V. T. (2012) Dancing in the wind. *Topos,* 79, pp. 21–29.

INDEX

First published in 2024 by
The Crowood Press Ltd
Ramsbury, Marlborough
Wiltshire SN8 2HR

www.crowood.com
enquiries@crowood.com

British Library Cataloguing-in-Publication Data
A catalogue record for this book is available from the British Library.

ISBN 978 0 7198 4389 1

Cover design: Sergey Tsvetkov
Front cover image: With special thanks to the Provost and Fellows of The Queen's College
Back cover image (top): The Grasslands Garden at the Horniman Museum designed by James Hitchmough with Wes Shaw

Dedication
For Ellie and Beth

Catherine Heatherington has asserted her right under the Copyright, Designs and Patents Act 1988 to be identified as the author of this work.

Typeset by SJmagic DESIGN SERVICES, India
Printed and bound in India by Thomson Press India Ltd

Acknowledgements

Thank you to my good friends and family, Larry, Ellie, Beth, Sergio and Jenny for their support. And a heart-felt thanks to my friend, colleague, and fellow writer, Alex Johnson, who has not only spent many hours discussing plants and design with me, but let me use one of her beautiful plans and several of her photos.

Several colleagues have been kind enough to talk about their work with me – John Little, Charlie Harpur, Vicky Wyer, Errol Fernandes and Rafia Sultana Hogg. And I would especially like to thank Philippa O'Brien, Rachel Bailey and Ed O'Brien, who have been generous enough to contribute details and photos of their designs.

All the photos were taken by me, unless other-wise stated. Thank you to the other photographers who kindly allowed me to use their work: Marianne Majerus, Clive Nichols, Sergio Denche, Ellie Mindel, Oli Holmes, Rosemary Lee, Alex Johnson, Ed O'Brien and Rachel Bailey.

Finally, I am very grateful to my clients, especially Sharon, the RSPB and the Queen's College, who have allowed me to indulge in my love of plants and wildlife when creating gardens for them.

Contributors

Alex Johnson's love of gardens and natural land-scapes has informed her wide-ranging landscape design practice for over four decades.

Rachel Bailey runs an award-winning practice based in Scotland creating plant-filled gardens, which are good for people and wildlife, and that aim to have a low environmental impact.
www.rachelbaileydesign.co.uk
Insta: rachel_bailey_garden.design

Ed O'Brien is a Bristol-based garden designer who specialises in drought-tolerant and ecological planting.
www.edobrien.co.uk

Philippa O'Brien is a London-based garden designer.
www.pipobriengardendesign.com